IMMENSE MISSED OPPORTUNITIES - **IMO**

IMMENSE MISSED OPPORTUNITIES - IMO

The Untapped Potential Available to
Help Solve World Problems

By
Helene Ballmann Dudley

A PEACE CROPS WRITERS BOOK
2023
OAKLAND, CALIFORNIA

Immense Missed Opportunities – IMO

The Untapped Potential Available to Help Solve World Problems

A Peace Corps Writers Book – an imprint of Peace Corps Worldwide

Printed in the United States of America
By Peace Corps Writers of Oakland, California

For more information, contact peacecorpsworldwide@gmail.com.
Peace Corps Writers and the Peace Corps Writers colophon are trademarks of PeaceCorpsWorldwide.org

ISBN-13: 978-1-950444-67-0
Library of Congress Control Number: 978-1-950444-67-0
First Peace Corps Writers Edition, October 2023

This book is dedicated to Innocent Ajaga and the women Rotarians of Yumbe, Uganda, who inspire me with their tireless and highly effective work in "Caring for Humanity," a motto emblazoned on the back of their Rotary shirts.

WORDS OF PRAISE FOR TCP GLOBAL AND IMMENSE MISSED OPPORTUNITIES – IMO

I read Helene Dudley's *Immense Missed Opportunities* as the nation rolled out below me on a flight from Boston to San Francisco. As one of the micro finances pioneers, I am disheartened when I visit villages in the developing world and find six or even ten Micro Finance Institutions making high-cost loans to the same people. Too often, they become snarled in debt, often taking out new loans to pay off old ones. Meanwhile, each MFI is making a buck off the backs of the poor. This is not the "silver bullet to end poverty" we were promised.

In *Immense Missed Opportunities*, Helene Dudley makes me believe in the potential of microfinance again. The starting point is saving in small groups. Once a cluster of groups has successfully saved and made loans, they contribute $1,500 to a loan fund matched by TCP. With more capital, they can grow their business. As they pay back their loans, the fund is recycled into more loans for more villagers. The fund is managed collectively by local leaders, not the paid staff of institutions who live away from the village. The impact on business growth supported by local communities is impressive.

Helene Dudley presents a low-cost, locally controlled, simple, extraordinarily low-cost, and highly replicable model of "financial inclusion" that represents a modest yet powerful antidote to the top-down, centralized and expensive alternatives so often touted as "solutions."

I can't recommend Helene's book more highly.

Jeffrey Ashe, Adjunct Associate Professor, Columbia University
Author of *In Their Own Hands: How Savings Groups are Revolutionizing Development*
Director, Grassroots Finance Action

Immense Missed Opportunities explains why and how TCP Global works with microloan groups, especially groups of rural women. As someone who has worked in impoverished countries since 1973, I find the effects astonishing. In most so-called "development programs," an external agency controls the money, hires and manages staff, and evaluates results. In the method that Dudley explains, the impoverished lead the planning, management, and evaluation. That is development. Specifically, the groups loan and repay the money responsibly. As the book states, the women increase their profits, pay back their loans with interest, keep their daughters and other children in school, improve their health, housing and communities, and become empowered to improve their communities. The microloan groups result in real development at extremely low input costs.

Chris Roesel. Founder and President – People to People (P2P),
Author of *How to Improve the World Quickly*
TCP Global Director for Africa Programs

No country can functionally develop when its women and youths are left behind. Helene Dudley created a culture of humanitarian service with the highest and most consistent standards of social concern. Her tireless efforts to support and improve the lives of marginalized and underdeveloped communities in Uganda and Yumbe District, in particular, have created a powerful movement in charity and service in Rotary that has championed the uplift of our people and countless others elsewhere in Africa. This profoundly useful book embodies the ideal of sheer, unadulterated humanitarian excellence.

Avako Melsa. Woman Member of Parliament
from Yumbe District, Uganda

TCP has changed my community. Before, women were not respected, they had no say in the community, and domestic violence was the order of the day, but with TCP Global, women are fully respected and have a full voice in the community and no violence. The community stays in peace, and the men normally say that the government of today is for women because everything favors women – women own businesses, own land, ride motorcycles, pay kids to school and take full control of home. Amazingly, women have a lot of money.

Rukia Driciru,
Founding member and first president of the
Rotary Club of Yumbe, Uganda

Development at the grassroots can only be better, faster and more sustainable when you involve the people themselves in solving their problem. Oftentimes, people know what works best but may not have the means to achieve the goal. The Community in Yumbe has been impacted by global challenges, including wars and conflicts in Uganda and South Sudan, resulting in being refugees at one time and now hosting refugees from Southern Sudan. The communities have proved that with a little push from a partner like TCP Global that offered microloans, they can identify viable solutions to their own problems as long as they are empowered with the relevant knowledge, attitude, skill and appropriate technology to transform the communities to greater developments.

Royce Gloria Androa
Vice Chair, Agency for Accelerated Rural Development,
AFARD, Uganda

The developing world is full of entrepreneurs and visionaries who, with access to education, equity and credit, would play a key role in developing the economic situation in their countries.

Muhammad Yunus

CONTENTS

INTRODUCTION

Immense Missed Opportunities IMO draws on my twenty-three years of experience building zero-overhead, sustainable micro-loan programs in marginalized communities around the world virtually, seated at my computer. What this experience has taught me is that instead of spending billions of dollars sending "experts" from developed nations to implement health, education, environment, and empowerment programs, there is an opportunity for better, faster, and more sustainable results. This can be achieved by investing a tiny fraction of the amount we currently spend to empower impoverished entrepreneurs living in those communities. And that is the premise of this book.

There are people within marginalized communities who know what is needed and how to achieve it. They simply need the resources to do it. With as little as $300 each, the entrepreneurs can increase their business earnings, eliminate hunger in their families, and have funds to keep their kids in school. In my experience, many of these empowered entrepreneurs then take on community problems themselves. There is no shortage of wisdom and initiative in poor communities. There is primarily a lack of resources.

Much has been written regarding the need to empower grassroots leadership, yet we cling to traditional models developed in first-world capitals. Those traditional models make sense in theory, but they underperform. Continuing to use them is the definition of insanity: repeating the same actions and expecting different results. For fear of making six-figure funding mistakes in trying something new, we continue to fund seven and eight-figure projects that too often exacerbate the plight of the poor.

There is a Better Way

There is an alternative, and IMO shows the way. Small loans allow micro-entrepreneurs to expand their businesses, escape abject poverty, and provide opportunities to a long chain of entrepreneurs as repayments are continuously reinvested in new loans. Economically empowered entrepreneurs often become leaders who help to uplift entire communities. This book will introduce you to some of them.

Starting with one $300 loan in Bogota, Colombia, in 2000, The Colombia Project went on to provide loans to impoverished entrepreneurs throughout Colombia before evolving in 2015 as TCP Global and supporting $1.5 million in loans in 2022, always working under the umbrella of a fiscal sponsor.

In 2022 alone, with just over $275,000 in outside funding, TCP Global supported 7,000 loans worth $1.5 million on three continents. We lack the bandwidth to track all the ripple effects of these loans, but in the Yumbe District of Northern Uganda, empowered borrowers, who no longer had to struggle to meet basic family needs, proceeded to adopt a village to reduce preventable diseases significantly. They also implemented prenatal services and monitoring of newborns in multiple villages. People who can survive on less than $2 per day are problem solvers of necessity. They are ready to take on the world when they suddenly have $5 per day.

IMO is written for anyone interested in reducing global poverty or better understanding why poverty persists. While most books on this subject are written from a policy-level perspective, IMO draws from experiences at the grassroots level. It identifies opportunities we are missing to empower people, like those in Yumbe, to maximize their potential.

Zambian economist, Dr. Dambisa Moyo, in her 2009 book *Dead Aid: Why Aid Is Not Working and How There is a Better Way for Africa,* explains why multi-million-dollar aid packages, as they are currently disbursed, are harmful. There has been a lot of soul-searching since she wrote her book, and literature abounds on the value of giving all stakeholders a place at the table, but understanding and implementing are two different things.

Similarities of Macro and Micro Levels

Dr. Moyo writes, "Our ability to create and sustain economic growth is the defining challenge of our time," which is equally true at the micro level for subsistence farmers and market vendors as at the macro level on Wall Street. At the grassroots, sustainable development originates within the self-same community, but people cannot plan for tomorrow when their families don't have enough to eat today. Once the entrepreneurial poor are empowered economically, many are prepared to lead the way.

IMO shows that what is learned at the macro level can inform actions at the micro level and vice-versa. The book also highlights benefits to the planet when we extend opportunities beyond the ranks of the privileged. Those on the front lines in the fight against poverty, food insecurity, climate change, and economic migration know a lot about what needs to be done, and they are capable of taking the lead, if a few development dollars come their way.

To show that this is truly an immense opportunity and there is a wealth of talent prepared to contribute to creating a more just and equitable society, IMO includes numerous examples of people from marginalized populations vastly exceeding expectations when given resources and support. These examples include school children in Haiti, Colombia, and Niger, former foster youth in Miami, as well as market vendors and subsistence farmers in Uganda overcoming the odds to achieve success.

Unlearning 'Truths'

In my 70s, I am unlearning much of what I was taught to be true during the first six decades of my life. It gives me hope. I have learned that conventional beliefs have many things backward, for example, that acquiring wealth requires wisdom and that rich, therefore, implies smart; that Western Christian values are superior; that we need to teach "them" how to be more like "us." I now realize it is more important for marginalized people to be heard than for them to hear what "experts" have to say.

IMO explains what distinguishes TCP Global from predatory micro-lending. Intentionality is critically important. TCP Global and its grassroots partners are motivated not by profit but by the desire to help people improve their lives. Working collaboratively, we have a track record of helping impoverished entrepreneurs increase their income and implement their plans to improve the quality of life for their families: pay school fees, improve nutrition, improve family dwellings, and create healthy environments.

What I Hope You Take Away From IMO

Throwing money at a problem may make that problem worse. Instead, we need to identify and address the root cause of the problem, which often is a lack of resources. By economically empowering people and programs already adding value to the community and working with them to build on their skills and by building on existing programs, better and more sustainable results are possible.

This book seeks to help readers understand why inclusion is in the best interest of our planet. It showcases successful efforts to empower positive, sustainable improvements that benefit people and the environment. Those successful efforts primarily focus on impoverished entrepreneurs, which admittedly excludes millions of needy individuals. This is a triage approach. From outside the community, we cannot help everyone, but if we empower local entrepreneurs, we will likely find that many become agents of change. They don't need outside experts to show the way; they just need the resources to implement what they see as best for their communities. In summary, by empowering the silent poor of the world, we bring millions more problem-solvers and producers to the table.

Know Your Values

This is liberating. As Pope Francis declared in rescinding the Doctrine of Discovery in early 2023, people in wealthy, developed nations are not called upon to teach the rest of the world what is in their best interest or help them adopt Western Christian values. Instead, we have the easier task of opening our minds and hearts to learn from others, recognizing them as equals, and working together in a respectful partnership.

TCP Global – Background

The Colombia Project began in 2000 with the assumption that the success of our micro-loan program hinged on our wisdom, guidance, and control. We quickly learned that success depended, instead, on finding the right partners, recognizing their wisdom, and making our model sufficiently flexible so partners could manage their programs as they saw fit.

Rather than setting up a costly process to exercise control, we opted to trust our partner's judgment and then verify the results. In 23 years, only two sites betrayed our trust and failed to invest funds as agreed. While both the betrayals and the $3,000 loss were painful, it was a small price to pay for the time, energy, and resources we saved by delegating control. If we had maintained control over the money and decision-making, our partners would not have grown into the powerful actors they have become, and there is no guarantee our results would have equaled or surpassed those achieved by our partners.

We verify results by tracking the loan activity funded by our donated dollars, using a monthly Excel report Sister Ruby in Genova, Colombia, developed to replace our more complicated form. This verification process helped us spot problems and close sites that charged high interest or failed to keep funds fully invested. By any international aid standards, even TCP Global's closed sites were resounding successes since, on average, they invested each donated dollar as requested, not once but more than three times.

Good Partners Are Essential

TCP Global finds good partners already working effectively in small communities referred by Returned Peace Corps Volunteers and Rotarians with personal knowledge of those partners. We also receive referrals from existing loan partners. These partners are willing to go the extra mile to add a small loan program to benefit their constituents.

Due to the high demand for our support, as of 2021, partners provide the first $1500 to start a small micro-loan program, which we monitor virtually through monthly email reports. After the first $1500 is invested twice in loans, we send another $1500 and continue sending funds until they have a revolving loan pool sufficient to meet the ongoing micro-loan needs of the community. The partner keeps the interest earnings to support small community projects.

TCP Global funds are, in essence, a grant to a community to set up a permanent loan program. Once funds enter the community, they stay in the community. Within two to three years, a loan pool is fully funded, and TCP Global moves on to support new communities. This self-sustainability distinguishes TCP Global from other micro-loan programs, like KIVA, which continue only as long as there is the infrastructure to support it and do not always reinvest loan payments in new loans.

My experience with TCP Global partners gives me reason to be optimistic. Human resources are the most valuable and precious natural resources we possess. In our partners and in the entrepreneurs who receive TCP Global loans through those partners, I see an abundance of largely untapped talent, wisdom and energy ready, willing, and capable of taking on the problems facing our world. The first step is to remove obstacles that prevent that talent from achieving its potential. They need resources.

CHAPTER 1

TALENT IS UNIVERSAL, OPPORTUNITY IS NOT

It is to everyone's benefit to unleash that untapped talent.

> "The developing world is full of entrepreneurs and visionaries, who with access to education, equity and credit would play a key role in developing the economic situations in their countries."
> *Muhammad Yunus, 2006 Nobel Peace Prize awardee for his work with micro-credit.*

My Breakthrough Moment

The NETFLIX documentary, *The Boy Who Harnessed the Wind,* provided an 'Aha!' moment for me. It's the story of a 13-year-old boy in Malawi whose family could not pay his school fees. The boy broke into the school library at night to learn how to build a windmill, which ultimately saved his family and his village from the drought that killed the crops. It made me wonder how much society was missing from other brilliant young minds who were denied the education they eagerly desired.

That little boy, William, went on to earn a bachelor's degree in environmental studies at Dartmouth University and is now working with the Moving Windmills Project to build an Innovation Center in Malawi where young people can find tools and mentorship to co-create simple solutions to everyday agricultural challenges.

While William, fortunately, did not slip through the cracks, there are countless others whose potential is lost to the world, like a starfish trapped on the beach by a broken system that may keep some of our best minds out of the arena, marooned in poverty.

During a 2007 visit to a friend working as a U.N. peacekeeper in Saint-Marc, Haiti, I saw that it took a positive attitude plus an inordinate amount of ingenuity, initiative, and hard work to survive in Haiti. I wondered if Haiti might have the strongest gene pool on the planet. What if the smartest people were not, after all, those born to privilege, sent to the best schools, and who then progressed to a life of abundance?

What if the voices of the rich and well-connected are not the ones most needed to guide us in sustaining life on the planet? What if *less* really is *more,* and we need input from those who know how to live on the absolute minimum of the world's resources – those who know how to survive on less than $2 per day?

Whether dealing with powerless people or dysfunctional countries, we find it all too easy to dismiss and even blame the victim rather than acknowledge their capability or accept any responsibility for the victim's plight. I believe we miss significant opportunities by ignoring the talent and potential of Haiti and Haitians, for example. They have much to offer the world if given a chance.

When AIDS and tuberculosis wracked Haiti in the late Twentieth Century, the last Dr. Paul Farmer of Partners in Health ignored all the nay-sayers who insisted poor people in Haiti could not take medicines as prescribed. They said it was a waste of resources to treat AIDS patients in Haiti. Because poor Haitians didn't have watches, how could they know when to take scheduled doses? We are too quick to discount the potential of people who do not look like or live like us. Conventional 'wisdom' recommended that HIV-AIDS programs in places like Haiti focus exclusively on prevention, leaving millions in impoverished communities around the world excluded from treatment programs.

Dr. Farmer set out to prove them wrong, and in 1998, he launched the HIV Equity Initiative to train community health workers to provide free treatment to HIV patients in marginalized communities. Within months, patients gained weight, and the death rate declined. The HIV Equity Initiative in Haiti became a model for disease treatment in all communities. According to research conducted by Weill Cornell Medical Researchers and published in 2016, AIDS survival rates in Haiti equaled those of the U.S. despite Haiti's abject poverty and political instability.[1] No doubt Haitians and other people living in similarly impoverished countries can show the way in other areas if given half a chance.

Wealth is not a measure of ability as much as a measure of privilege. The poor may have abilities that could help all of us if they did not need to use all their energy and skill to survive. What if we removed obstacles from their paths so that family survival no longer consumes all their energy? If they were freed to devote their talents to common problems, what life-changing, planet-saving innovations could they bring to the table? In Haiti's case, some will suggest that if talent existed in Haiti, it would have prevented the country from becoming the most fragile state in the Western Hemisphere and 11th in the world[2]. Well, Haiti didn't become dysfunctional by accident.

Background on Poverty in Haiti

In a Planet Money segment on National Public Radio (NPR), Greg Rosalfsky noted that "Haiti is one of the poorest nations in the world, and rich countries have their fingerprints all over the

1 Drs. Samuel Pierre et al. "Haitian AIDS patients' 10 year Survival Equal to American Patients." (Weill Cornell Newsroom, January 27, 2016) https://news.weill.cornell.edu/news/2016/01/haitian-aids-patients-10-year-survival-equal-to-american-patients

2 https://en.wikipedia.org/wiki/List_of_countries_by_Fragile_States_Index.

nation's stunted development."[3] After fighting 13 years to become, in 1804, only the second independent nation in the Americas, Haiti was soon forced, at gunpoint, by French battleships to compensate France for the land and slaves lost in the rebellion. Imagine if the 13 U.S. colonies had been required to pay England for the land colonists had just fought and died for during the Revolutionary War.

Why was Haiti penalized economically for its successful revolution? Slave-owning countries, including the United States, feared that a successful Haiti might encourage other slaves to contemplate rebellion. While the American colonies were aided in their struggle against England by Spain, France, and the Netherlands, among others, powerful nations set out to ensure that Haiti would fail. The economic burden imposed by France and condoned by other Western nations deprived Haiti of the financial resources to build a viable society.

Haiti thus became the only country in history where descendants of enslaved peoples paid reparations to descendants of their former masters. Over the course of 122 years, through 1947, Haiti paid France the 21st-century equivalent of between 20 and 30 billion U.S. dollars.[4]

Some might argue that was long ago and not connected to Haiti's present-day problems. They would be wrong. Haiti suffered long-term impacts from the lack of education and infrastructure as a direct result of France's economic stranglehold.

As if the French diversion of wealth were not enough, in 1914, while Haiti was still paying France, U.S. marines confiscated Haiti's national gold reserves, worth $13.5M in 2022 dollars and occupied Haiti for two decades. And there is more. The brutal, if staunchly, anti-communist regimes of Papa Doc and Baby

---

3 Greg Rosalfsky, "The Greatest Heist in History: How Haiti was Forced to Pay Reparations for Freedom." WLRN, NPR, Planet Money, October 5, 2021 10:25 a.m.https://www.npr.org/sections/money/2021/10/05/1042518732/-the-greatest-heist-in-history-how-haiti-was-forced-to-pay-reparations-for-freed

4 New York Times May, 2022 series on Haiti

Doc Duvalier were propped up by U.S. foreign aid dollars. Those dollars, ostensibly to improve education, health, roads, and overall living conditions for Haiti's poor, were used instead to terrorize and subdue the population and strengthen the Duvaliers' brutal, thieving dictatorships. The Duvaliers and their circle of supporters pocketed the aid dollars.

I have traveled in some remote areas in Mexico, Guatemala, Uganda, and Cambodia but have never seen roads in such horrible condition as the ones I traveled in Haiti in 1992 and 2007, which, I was told, had not been repaired since before the Duvalier regimes. It is hard to develop a country with no viable road network. To make matters worse, Haitian intelligentsia fled the brutal dictatorship, depriving Haiti of not only financial resources but key human resources as well.

Blaming the victim

History is written by the rich and powerful, which does not include Haiti, whose successful fight for independence against France was largely suppressed from the news at the time. Today, Haiti is dismissed as a failed state, plagued by corruption and violence, which, stripped from the backstory, leaves the impression the fault lies with the Haitian people, who must be less capable than other populations, which is far from the truth.

To survive in a society battered by history and ravaged by earthquakes and hurricanes takes an inordinate amount of fortitude, initiative, and hard work. It's easy to succeed when you are born on third base but far more challenging if you are still in the batter's box with a sprained ankle, a cracked bat, and a three-run deficit. Imagine how much better Haiti, our hemisphere, and possibly the world would be if Haiti had been allowed to develop its talent and thrive like other newly independent countries.

Welcome HELP

One of the places I visited in 2007 was the Haitian Education and Leadership Program (HELP) office in Port-au-Prince. In my opinion, HELP embodies the premise of this book – that society has much to gain by removing obstacles that prevent talented people (or nations) from achieving their potential.

Twenty-five years ago, a Peace Corps language instructor in Haiti started out to help just one young lady, the equivalent of releasing just one starfish into the ocean. "HELP began with a single donation that provided tuition and books for a promising young Haitian woman with a dream of studying medicine. Growing up, this young woman was so poor that she sometimes couldn't afford to eat. When she and her family visited the local clinic, the staff treated them poorly because of their circumstances, so she imagined starting her own clinic where all patients would be regarded with kindness and respect.

Thanks to the donation from her English teacher, HELP founder Conor Bohan, that young woman—Dr. Isemonde Joseph—was able to complete her medical degree in 2005. She went on to work at a clinic in Port-Au-Prince, where she treats patients with compassionate skill."[5]

Twenty-five years later, HELP alumni comprise a new middle class of leaders devoted to reforming Haiti. They have built libraries, affordable housing, nonprofits, and small businesses through their initiatives, creating opportunities for their peers while promoting a more just and empathic society. Their collaborative attitude is a model for citizenship in their communities.

Over the last 25 years, HELP has:

1. Educated 280 scholars, 80% of whom still reside in Haiti (the reverse of the national average for educated Haitians),
2. Produced 6 Fulbright scholars,
3. Maintained a 99% program retention rate,
4. Prepared its graduates to earn over 13 times the average annual Haitian salary ($9800 vs. $743).

5 https://www.uhelp.net/en/about.

With more funds, HELP could support more Haitian scholars. According to their website:

"HELP's mission is to create, through merit and needs-based scholarships, a community of young professionals and leaders who will promote a more just society in Haiti. We envision a Haiti where every Haitian has access to quality education, the opportunity to live up to his or her potential, and the ability to contribute to a just and prosperous society." It is impossible to right the wrongs of the past, but HELP, in educating a new class of talented leaders, creates opportunities for Haiti to mend itself, free from the meddling of outsiders with their own agendas.

Hope for Haiti

In my opinion, the HELP model provides the greatest hope for Haiti for building a strong, educated, civic-minded middle class capable of lifting the country from within. Haiti needs all hands on deck, and we are currently missing opportunities to empower many bright young Haitians, like Jacques Kelly Durandisse, whose single mother worked as a domestic cook but was often unable to put food on the table for her own children. Jacques says, "The HELP scholarship made life immediately easier. It covered all my daily needs like food, laundry, housing, supplies, and books, and I was better prepared to address academic challenges once my basic needs were met".[6] He more than met those challenges, consistently ranking in the top five of his class of over 100. He now works for the local water department and teaches the community how to harness the environment for sustainable economic and ecological development."

Valencia Brutus grew up in Cité Soleil, an extremely impoverished and densely populated area in Port-au-Prince and is now a role model for that community. "Now my neighbors want their children to go to school, study hard, and become someone who can contribute to our society. Education is the way to succeed," she said.

6 https://www.uhelp.net/en/alumni.

Ronel LeFranc was the first in his family to finish high school. A HELP scholarship gave him the support he needed to study at the university, where he learned of Haiti's brain drain. "We talked about how over 80% of educated Haitian professionals are living abroad, so when you look at Haiti, you see a real leadership crisis. We are the citizens of this country, and we are the ones who must take care of it. No one else is going to do it for us." After completing his university education, he obtained a Master's degree in Global Development at St. John's University and then became assistant program director for an NGO that works with locals on a holistic approach to community development. Ronel is also the CEO and co-founder of ACTIVEH, a pan-university civic organization that provides internships, professional development, and networking.

The IMO Insight: Talent Is Everywhere

We might think ourselves immune (to this), but we are not. We are missing opportunities to develop talent in the U.S., as well. Poverty is part of the problem, but foster youth face extra challenges. When foster children turn 18, they are typically emancipated from state custody, which brings the end of state support. An 18-year-old with a solid foundation and a helpful network of friends, family, and advisors would likely find it difficult to manage housing, food, health care, and the myriad other responsibilities of adult life. Children in the foster care system do not have a solid foundation, having experienced multiple disruptions in their education while simultaneously trying to cope with the dissolution of their family connection and adjusting to a series of foster families.

Small wonder that 70% of the California prison population are products of the foster care system, 75% in Connecticut and 80% in Illinois, according to 1995 data.[7] According to a 2016 Bureau of Justice survey, the situation has improved but is still alarming. "Close to one-fifth of the prison population in the U.S. comprises former foster children."[8]

---

7 https://adoptioninchildtime.org/bondingbook/striking-back-in-anger-delinquency-and-crime-in-foster-children.

8 Bureau of Justice Statistics (BJS) (2016), Survey of prison inmates.

It Doesn't Have to Be This Way

What if state governments provided meaningful support through that transition period to adulthood? Instead of ending financial support for foster youth at age 18 and waiting for them to return to state care as part of the prison population, costing taxpayers over $35,000 per prisoner per year[9], why not invest a little up front to give foster kids an opportunity to create a better future for themselves?

The State of Florida has a tuition exemption program for former foster children and also provides a monthly living allowance if they are enrolled in any post-secondary studies, from beautician schools to four-year universities. Texas and California also have tuition waivers for foster kids. The problem is that foster kids experience so many rejections and disappointments in life they have trouble believing that something good can happen to them. They may assume they do not qualify if they know about the programs.

EDUCATE TOMORROW - Mentoring Program that Develops Potential

Virginia Emmons, founder and the first CEO of Educate Tomorrow, launched the program with support from her sisters when she realized how few foster children availed themselves of a life-changing opportunity. According to the Educate Tomorrow website,

> "Young adults from foster care could receive free college tuition in Florida, and yet very few were accessing this benefit. In 2003, only eight students were reported using the Florida Department of Child and Families (DCF) tuition exemption program for universities.
>
> We thus began to play a significant role in increasing the number of scholars who became aware of and used the tuition

---

9 Federal Register, Annual Determination of Average Cost of Incarceration Fee (COIF), 9/1/2021. https://www.federalregister.gov/documents/2021/09/01/2021-18800/annual-determination-of-average-cost-of-incarceration-fee-coif.

exemption program. By 2019, there were 6,700 students accessing the benefit. Our first college coaching program in 2013, along with education and outreach to other institutions, contributed to accelerated growth."[10]

Educate Tomorrow mentors become involved when their mentees are still in foster care, helping them navigate the system to apply for further education. Mentors give their mentees the encouragement they need to persevere. Having one person who believes in you and encourages you can make all the difference. "Nationally, 3% - 11% of youth from the foster care system graduate from college, while, in the last five years, over 90% of foster system alumni mentored by Educate Tomorrow persisted to earn a college degree."

As a child-neglect social worker in Chicago, I witnessed first-hand the many obstacles faced by foster children whose home and school lives were repeatedly disrupted. If "That which does not kill you makes you stronger" turns out to be true, then foster kids have the potential to be among the strongest. It behooves society to provide them with the incentive and the tools to use those strengths in productive ways.

There is a missed opportunity here to redirect disaffected young people from the path of hopelessness that leads to prison and guide them along the path to becoming productive citizens. The benefits to society would be significant in economic terms, considering that, nationwide, 69% of those who age out of the foster care system are incarcerated at least once by age 26[11]. The benefits to the individual are life-changing, as Kendricka's story on the Educate Tomorrow website exemplifies.

"When Kendricka showed up at Educate Tomorrow's door, she had lost hope. Her drug-addicted mother had abandoned her and her three younger sisters, forcing Kendricka to drop out of high school to care for them. She said the police would

---

10 https://www.educatetomorrow.org.

11 Courtney, M, A Dworsky, A Brown, C Cary, K Love, V Vorhies and C Hall), "Midwest evaluation of the adult functioning of former foster youth: Outcomes at age 26." (Chicago, Chapin Hall at the University of Chicago, 2011), 92

> routinely show up to evict the girls and place them in foster homes, but she hid with her sisters under the bed. 'I knew if we went to foster care, I would age out before they did. And I couldn't live with that. Most people didn't think I was gonna make it this far. At 16, even I didn't see making it to 18. When I tried to picture my life in two years, for some reason, it was a total blank. I could see nothing I had to offer the world.'"

Fortunately, through her relationship with her mentor at Educate Tomorrow, Kendricka was able to create a future for herself. "I kept asking my mentor how she did these amazing things, traveling all over the world, doing work she loved. She kept repeating, 'Education is the key, education is the key.'"

Saving Lives and Saving Money

Educate Tomorrow is prepared to replicate its program in more states. Currently, Texas, California, and Florida have state-funded tuition waivers for former foster youth and have Educate Tomorrow programs. While the state of Colorado does not have a tuition waiver, a private foundation agreed to cover the costs so that Colorado, too, has a branch of Educate Tomorrow. For other states, this is a tremendous missed opportunity to do the right thing for a marginalized population while saving the state large sums of money each year by reducing incarceration.

Education is the Key

Kendricka's mentor spoke the truth when she said, "Education is the key." If we provide opportunities so that young people can achieve their potential, hopelessness and crime will decline. Netflix has numerous documentaries about kids from poor areas outperforming their wealthier counterparts. Just imagine what they have to offer the world.

More proof that talent is universal, though opportunity is not, comes from a Colombia Peace Corps site. As a Peace Corps Volunteer in a small rural community in the mountains overlooking Medellin, Colombia, in the 1960s, Maureen Orth started a school.

In 2005, she was contacted by the school, which by then had been named after her, and was asked to help prepare its students for the 21st century. In response, she created The Marina Orth Foundation with the tagline "Educating for the Future." They now have 21 schools in marginalized neighborhoods in and around Medellin where K-11 children receive computers, learn English and leadership, focus on STEM curriculum, and begin coding from an early age.

Robotics

Robotics clubs inspire big dreams and provide the tools to realize those dreams. In 2018, their all-girls robotics team won a gold medal at RoboRAVE in Albuquerque, New Mexico, beating the boys' teams from China, Japan, the U.S., and many other countries. In 2019, three Marina Orth program teenagers were invited to participate in one of the world's most prestigious robotics competitions, ROBOTEX INTERNATIONAL, held in Tallinn, Estonia. Although they did not win in Tallinn, they received scholarships through the Marina Orth Foundation to study computer science and architecture at one of Medellin's most prestigious universities.[12]

The impact of the Marina Orth programs extends beyond the individual students. Two months after winning in Medellin, two Orth Foundation robotics teams headed to South Korea in the summer of 2023, where they would place 3rd, competing against the brightest minds of their generation.

The mother of one participant noted how this had brought their community together. "We became a single family on this adventure together - we learned how to work as a team, dream together, ... laugh and pull together for the same dream... a united family achieves great things. The Marina Orth Foundation helped our village to climb to another level, allowing children and young people to have another vision of the world, allowing them to envision a better future. Doña Marina has brought a light of hope ... that has touched the soul of many boys and girls."

12 https://www.fundaorth.org/4ward/.

Desiring a better future for children is a universal value most parents link to education. Roughly the same time when Maureen Orth responded to the call for education from her former Peace Corps site in the mountains outside Medellin, newly arrived Peace Corps Volunteer Virginia Emmons arrived on the other side of the world to the hot and dusty village of Kabey Fo, Niger. This is the same Virginia who later founded Educate Tomorrow. Virginia was overwhelmed by both the heat and the multiple immediate needs she saw in her village, but when asked, village leaders looked to the future and said they wanted education for their children.

Loans Provide Resources to Invest in the Future

Families across Africa make educating the next generation a priority, but making education a priority and having the resources to invest in education are two different things. TCP Global micro-loans give entrepreneurs the means to increase their earnings so that education becomes a reality. During my 2022 visit to Uganda, borrowers consistently told me they used the increased earnings resulting from micro-loan investments in business improvements to pay school fees.

My experience is consistent with findings of the April 2019 USAID Village Savings and Loan Association Assessment, which reported that "The three most commonly cited reasons for taking out loans among the VSLA groups interviewed include (in order of frequency mentioned): 1) paying school fees, 2) investing in business, and 3) farming."[13]

Obstacles to Success

The entrepreneurial poor struggle to do what they know they need to do to get ahead, but they could do much better if society only removed the obstacles in their path. Families in Yumbe, Uganda, spend 20% to 40% of their income treating malaria, which does not even begin to reflect the full economic impact of malaria on poor families. Missed days of work and school, for example,

13 USAID Village Savings and Loan Association Assessment (April, 2019), 15 https://pdf.usaid.gov/pdf_docs/PA00TRWH.pdf

result in reduced earnings. Meanwhile, Chris Roesel of People to People lobbied relentlessly for over a year to distribute some of the 34 million mosquito nets donated by the U.S. government that Malaria Partners International reports are sitting in Uganda warehouses. Chris was asked to stop contacting people at U.S. AID about this because "it made staff feel bad."

According to online research, mosquito nets were the best malaria prevention measure available at the time. The World Health Organization recommends insecticide-treated nets or ITNs. While waiting for nets to be released, a team of Rotarians in Yumbe is testing and treating entire villages in an attempt to wipe out all potential hosts for malaria in concentrated areas. They are planting mosquito-repellent vegetation and removing mosquito breeding grounds. They recently received a grant to fight malaria, but their request for mosquito nets was not funded because there are already 34 million nets in Uganda awaiting distribution. Whatever the cause of the holdup, and many have been suggested, until this is resolved, there is a huge missed opportunity to remove a major obstacle on the path to economic prosperity in Northern Uganda.

In late 2023, as this book was being prepared for publication, we learned that a malaria vaccine would become available in Uganda and several other African countries in the last quarter of the year.

Material Rewards in Knocking Down Social Barriers

A U.S. study completed by Researchers at the University of Chicago and Stanford University, published in the spring of 2012, measured the positive impact of removing barriers to previously marginalized groups. They found that "up to one-fifth of America's wage growth over the past 50 years can be attributed to the knocking down of social barriers that prevented women and minorities from doing their best--clearing the way for waitresses to become lawyers, or African-American orderlies to become doctors."[14] We can anticipate a similar rise in productivity by knocking down barriers for impoverished and otherwise marginalized people. To some degree, this is personal.

Great Society Programs Came Late to the U.S.

Upon viewing the Presidential Library display of social programs initiated during Lyndon B. Johnson's presidency, I imagined how different my parents' lives could have been if rural electrification, Medicare, Medicaid, and Johnson's various anti-poverty programs had been in place earlier. Despite ending his formal education in the 8th grade, my father remained a lifelong learner who questioned the status quo and devised ways to improve. He applied for patents for his double-headed nail, paint-can collar and a ground-soil coring instrument. He subscribed to *Organic Gardening* long before it was trendy and once told me, "If bugs don't eat it, I am not sure I want to eat it." He questioned the world around him. He worried about nuclear power and questioned the government enough that it may have triggered his tax audit during the Nixon years. One evening each week, he volunteered with the St. Vincent De Paul Society to help the less fortunate.

While struggling to raise a family in the post-war era, my parents and their siblings were the only safety net for their aging parents, pre-Great Society. In rural Missouri, my grandmother's house still had a well, a wood-burning stove and an outhouse when she died in the late 1950s. Life would have been very different had rural poverty been addressed earlier, particularly for my father. I often wonder where his inquisitiveness and creativity might have taken him had life given him more opportunities, fewer obstacles, and access to quality education. Individuals lose, but society also loses when we fail to provide opportunities for people to develop their talents.

---

14 Jim Tankersley, "The 100% Economy: Why the U.S. Needs a Strong Middle Class to Thrive." The Atlantic. (May 18, 2012) https://www.theatlantic.com/business/archive/2012/05/the-100-economy-why-the-us-needs-a-strong-middle-class-to-thrive/257385/

All Hands On-Deck to Address Global Problems

Our planet has serious problems – climate change, food insecurity, political upheavals, disinformation, rising seas, massive migration, pandemics, and extreme weather events. While it may have been possible in the past for the wealthiest to shield themselves from the consequences of global events, this is not the case now, especially for our children and grandchildren, barring some secret plan to relocate to a new planet. Our best chance is to share the wealth, share opportunities and enlist more people working on addressing our mutual problems.

Yes We Can

Some people say we cannot afford to mitigate the effects of climate change or reduce income inequality. In his book *A World of Three Zeros,* Dr. Muhammad Yunus explains how societies can prosper by reducing poverty, unemployment, and carbon emissions to zero. In her 2014 book, *This Changes Everything*, Naomi Klein says pretty much the same things as Dr. Yunus: "Klein meticulously builds the case for how massively reducing our greenhouse emissions is our best chance to simultaneously reduce gaping inequalities, re-imagine our broken democracies, and rebuild our gutted local economies."[15]

We do not have to pick and choose or prioritize. Doing the right thing for the environment can also correct income inequality. Former U.N. Secretary-General Ban-Ki Moon says the same thing: "Saving our planet, lifting people out of poverty, advancing economic growth. These are one and the same fight. We must connect the dots between climate change, water scarcity, energy shortages, global health, food security and women's empowerment. Solutions to one problem must be solutions for all."[16]

---

15 Simon & Schuster, "About the Book" https://www.simonandschuster.com/books/This-Changes-Everything/Naomi-Klein/9781451697391

16 Ban Ki-Moon, Address to the 66th General Assembly, "We the Peoples" (September 27, 2011) https://www.un.org/sg/en/content/sg/speeches/2011-09-21/address-66th-general-assembly-we-peoples

The prerequisite awareness, interest, and willingness to work for change are there. I was surprised to see market vendors in northern Uganda, one step removed from abject poverty, embrace "Caring for Humanity" as their Rotary Club motto and then go on to live by that. One of their groups is called "We Are Woken." They practice sustainable agriculture, plant trees, and treated COVID seriously. They are aware of what is going on in the world. Once their primary mission of feeding and educating their children was secured, they decided to help the less fortunate.

They chose one of the poorest villages in their region to eradicate malaria and water-borne illnesses and then moved on to adopt more villages. They appreciate what they are given and seek ways to pay it forward to help others. Is this universally true in marginalized communities? No, but common enough that it makes sense for those of us with means to seek ways to find and empower the altruistic and entrepreneurial poor. They are better equipped than the brightest minds from Oxford and Stanford to help their neighbors at a much lower cost.

The irony, of course, is that if we continue the current path, marginalized people currently surviving on next to nothing will be better prepared than the rest of us to survive climate disasters. They already know how to survive disasters with scarce resources. For the rest of us, it may well be an insurmountable challenge.

Small Loans and Waste Management for Kolibagonga Village ... July 20, 2023

Mokko, Niger, is in an arid region with few opportunities, especially in terms of women's access to finance. TCP Global loans address the financial service gap.

Families from 2 savings groups in Kolibagonga village in Mokko, collaborated in June on a waste composting and sanitation initiative for the village.

Excerpt from TCP Global newsletter of July 20, 2023

KOLI, a 34-member savings group in Kolibagonga, joined TCP Global in May, 2021

Mariama is a widow and head of household.

Thanks to her TCP Global loans, her business earnings have improved so she can adequately feed her children and grandchildren.

Balkissa used her loans to buy and raise goats.

Excerpt from TCP Global newsletter of July 20, 2023

Maimouna sells condiments, cassava flour, cowpea, and other items she buys wholesale to resell in her village. A TCP Global loan helped her increase inventory and earnings.

Mariama makes soumbala (a local spice) and makes mats, which she sells in the Balayara market every 2 - 3 weeks.

Maimona, the sole provider for her family, says TCP GLOBAL loans are a gift from God to wipe away her tears.

Thanks to loans for her small business she is able to care for her children and "make them smile."

Excerpt from TCP Global newsletter of July 20, 2023

CHAPTER 2

MIGRATION AS A CHOICE, NOT A NECESSITY

Bringing Opportunity to Small and Remote Communities

> "Look after the land, and the land will look after you, destroy the land, and it will destroy you." *Aboriginal Proverb*

In this chapter, we will explore how our inability to get services to rural areas contributes to urban and international migration and exacerbates food insecurity. This is partially due to hubris, assuming that Western minds with Western salaries need to be in control and since Western workers resist traveling to remote sites, those sites remain under-resourced. Meanwhile, there are talented people who, with minimal resources, could solve their problems and perhaps contribute to solving global problems as well.

In a December 2000 release entitled Rural Poverty in Developing Countries, the International Monetary Fund (IMF) reported, "Rural poverty accounts for nearly 63% of poverty worldwide, reaching 90% in some countries like Bangladesh and between 65% and 90% in sub-Saharan Africa. (Exceptions to this pattern are several Latin American countries where poverty is concentrated in urban areas.) In almost all countries, the conditions—in terms of personal consumption and access to education, health care, potable water and sanitation, housing, transport, and communications—faced by the rural poor are far worse than those faced by the urban poor. Persistently high levels of rural poverty, with or without overall economic growth, have contributed to rapid population growth and migration to urban areas. In fact, much urban poverty is created by the rural poor's efforts to get out of poverty by moving to cities."[17]

If we want to stem the flow of migration, a good place to start is to improve opportunities in rural areas. That same IMF report found that "In the community, minority ethnic or religious groups suffer more than majority groups, and the rural poor more than the urban poor; among the rural poor, landless wage workers suffer more than small landowners or tenants."

Little has changed since that 2000 IMF report. In a 2017 interview, Gilbert Houngbo, leader of the United Nations International Fund for Agricultural Development (IFAD), said, "Food security and nutrition are essential, but we have to go beyond that and really aim at the fight against poverty and look at agriculture as a decent income-generating activity. …Without adequate investment in the world's most vulnerable communities, there will be increased instability and conflict, and people will find it harder to bounce back from shocks, giving them more reasons to flee rural areas."[18]

We Suffer Enormously in Africa - Help Us

Dr. Dambisa Moyo prefaces her 2009 book *Dead Aid* with a "Message found on the bodies of Guinean teenagers Yaguine Kaita and Fode Tounkara, stowaways who died attempting to reach Europe in the landing gear of an airplane."[19] Their note read, "To

17 Mahmood Hasan Khan, "Rural Poverty in Developing Countries," Finance and Development - a quarterly magazine of the IMF, Volume 37, no 4 (December, 2000) https://www.imf.org/external/pubs/ft/fandd/2000/12/khan.htm.

18 Gilbert Houngbo, Interview published by UN IFAD, April 5, 2017 https://www.ifad.org/es/web/latest/-/story/in-conversation-with-ifad-s-new-president-gilbert-f-houngbo

19 Dambisa Moyo, "Dead Aid: Why Aid IS Not Working and How There is a Better Way for Africa," (New York: Farrar, Strauss and Giroux, 2009), preceding the Table of Contents

the Excellencies and officials of Europe: We suffer enormously in Africa. Help us. We have problems in Africa. We lack rights as children. We have war and illness. We lack food … We want to study, and we ask you to help us to study so we can be like you in Africa."

Yaguine and Fode were clear on what they sought, and it is a message we hear repeatedly from impoverished African parents who view education as the key to success for the next generation. They struggle to pay school fees, but children cannot study if their bellies ache from hunger, if they lose four to five hours each day fetching water, or if they are exhausted from fighting dysentery and diarrhea.

As Yaguine and Fode wrote, ambitious young people like them, living in communities plagued by war, famine, and disease and lacking water, electricity, and internet connectivity, need help, and they would prefer to get that help within Africa. In light of the billions of dollars in foreign aid dispensed in recent decades to Africa, it is easy to dismiss their pleas and miss their point by believing we have already helped them. *Dead Aid* outlines how the very opposite is true. At any rate, little of that aid reaches small and remote communities.

Failure to Help Small and Remote Communities

Sitting in one of many delightful cafes in Antigua, Guatemala, frequented by expats working for international development agencies, I tried to interest people in helping three Huehuetenango communities where TCP Global had microloan programs. A 10 or 12-hour drive by car, they said, was too far. The Peace Corps would not send volunteers there, adding that it was too dangerous; the same rationale that the Peace Corps office in Kampala stated for not sending volunteers 12 hours away to Yumbe in Northern Uganda – too far and too dangerous. There may well be significant security concerns for those areas, but the sad fact is that, despite billions in aid, communities most desperate for help are getting very little of the help they need. But when help arrives, results are often spectacular.

When Virginia Emmons arrived at her Niger Peace Corps site of Kabey Fo, which means 'one tree,' in 2000, there was not even one tree and no school. While Virginia could immediately see multiple things that this community of 200 desperately needed to make their lives healthier and more comfortable, in the short term, the villagers took the long view and asked for a school. They started with a one-room school in 2001 and gradually expanded to provide six years of primary education with an enrollment of 77 children. Virginia then negotiated with the government and Peace Corps to provide boarding facilities so Kabey Fo graduates could continue their secondary school studies. Kabey Fo achieved one of the highest school enrollment rates in Niger. Significant progress is possible when people define their own priorities.

Two organizations led by Returned Peace Corps Volunteer Rotarians, Chris Roesel and myself, work collaboratively with grassroots organizations in remote areas of Niger, the Democratic Republic of the Congo (DRC), and Uganda to address problems prioritized by the community with solutions developed in the community. Through our networks and drawing on more than sixty years of combined international development experience, Chris and I connect community leaders to the information they need and then help them find resources to achieve their goals.

The usual starting point is with TCP Global affordable loans so that micro-entrepreneurs may improve their businesses, increase their incomes, and care for their families' basic needs. In northern Uganda, that means putting children in better schools, buying land to build a permanent house, and providing three meals a day. At the same time that the loans directly benefit micro-entrepreneurs, the interest and other earnings from running the micro-loan program provide grassroots organizations a permanent revenue stream to invest in community improvement projects. The organization established by Chris, People to People (P2P), excels at identifying low-tech, low-cost, proven, sustainable ways to improve water, sanitation, and health. P2P also excels at listening to and respecting the people.

TCP Global+ is the long-term vision of TCP Global and P2P working together to help communities, particularly rural communities, become viable, so migration becomes a choice rather than a necessity. It starts with economic empowerment to help people develop the means to meet their basic needs and then progresses to eradicating the diseases that sap their strength and deplete their finances.

Resistance to Serving Remote Sites

Many Non-Governmental Organizations (NGOs) balk at even a 12-hour car ride to places served by TCP Global, like San Francisco Momonlac or Nueva Generación Maya, in Huehuetenango, Guatemala, or Yumbe in Uganda. For logical reasons, cities are magnets for goods, services, and capital, but this creates a disparity that does not serve the common good. Cities typically have difficulty assimilating rural migrants seeking those goods, services, and capital. Providing goods, services, and capital in remote locations will not only improve the quality of life in remote villages but will also reduce the negative impacts on cities unable to assimilate a high volume of migrants.

As people flee rural areas, there is a corresponding loss of farmers working the land to produce food. While industrialized agriculture has increased the quantity of food available, convincing research suggests that there has been a commensurate decline in food quality and soil quality, as well as adverse impacts on the environment. If those small farmers who prefer to stay on the land had the opportunity to earn a decent living off the land rather than become part of the migration problem, they could become part of the food scarcity solution.

A Sept. 13, 2021 report of the United Nations Food Programme entitled *9 Ways Food Systems Are Failing Humanity* found that "Humanity's food systems often emphasize quantity over quality, giving rise to a host of health and environmental concerns..."[20]

20 UN Environment Program "9 ways food systems are failing humanity" September 13, 2021 https://www.unep.org/news-and-stories/story/9-ways-food-systems-are-failing-humanity

Need for Regenerative Agriculture

Help is on the way. A September 2022 publication by Just Food, entitled "Why we're in a critical period in the development of regenerative agriculture," reports that corrective measures are being researched, implemented, and analyzed to reverse the negative impacts of industrialized agriculture. Major food distributors, such as Danone, PepsiCo, Nestle and General Mills, introduced incentives to their supply chains to pilot regenerative agriculture techniques.[21] In the long run, the right thing to do is projected to also be the profitable thing to do, but during the transition phase, industrialized agriculture's bottom line will likely take a hit, and productivity is likely to decrease with a corresponding rise in food prices. It will come as no surprise when the most vulnerable people on the planet suffer the harshest impacts of this transition.

The good news is that the most vulnerable people living close to the land are often among the most flexible and adaptable. A small-scale farmer can more easily transition to rotating land usage among various crops and farm animals, thereby preserving soil quality, which maintains food quality. It takes a special person who prefers a lifestyle close to the land, far from the faster-paced life of towns and cities. To the extent we find ways to support those special people, we serve the common good.

Improving Food Security

Numerous TCP Global partners promote regenerative agriculture to improve food security in impoverished areas. The website of TCP Global Kenya partner, Development in Gardening (DIG), proclaims, "A Better World is Rooted in Food. ... DIG improves the nutrition and livelihoods of uniquely marginalized communities by planting regenerative gardens that grow health, wealth, and a sense of belonging."[22]

---

21 David Burrows, "Why we're in a critical period in the development of regenerative agriculture," Just Food, September 21, 2022

22 Development in Gardening website, 2023, https://www.dig.org

Potentiel Terre (Earth Potential) in Niger works in more than 40 villages to increase food production in one of the poorest countries on earth, where malnutrition is one of the main reasons children miss school. Thanks to affordable loans funded through TCP Global, there are funds to implement improvements to increase agricultural production. In terms of the scale of food insecurity facing Niger, the TCP Global contribution is minuscule. But as in the story of the boy saving the starfish, what Potentiel Terre can accomplish with TCP Global funds makes a big difference to the villages they *can* help.

In Nepal, TCP Global is fortunate to work with Yogi Kayastha of Development Fund Norway. Yogi is willing to not only take those 12-hour bus rides but also take a daylong hike to reach remote sites. Development Fund Norway (DFN) funds community-based organizations (CBOs) in remote areas of Nepal to improve agriculture and animal husbandry and help people develop the skills they need to thrive. Finding the capital to implement the new skills was a challenge until TCP Global offered small, affordable loans to the people DFN trained.

Rural Opportunities - Reduced Migration

Like the women in Uganda, victims of caste discrimination in Nepal identify feeding and educating their children as their top priority. Too often, this requires male family members to emigrate to do dirty, dangerous, and demeaning jobs in neighboring countries. Some died building stadiums for the 2022 World Cup in Qatar. Others returned from Qatar but without promised salaries. Luckier ones found a way to stay home, with support from the Development Fund Norway's skills training and TCP Global micro-loans. They joined their wives to increase food production. Rather than contribute to migration, a world problem, with DFN training and TCP Global loans, they become part of the solution to food insecurity.

Pressure on MFIs to Reach Small and Remote Communities.

At the Microcredit Summit in Merida, Mexico, in 2014, there was an ongoing discussion of the need to make credit available in small and remote areas. There was considerable pressure on major Microfinance Institutions (MFIs) to find a way to serve those communities. At that time, Mexico was already extending micro-credit to a few remote communities but reported that the cost of servicing those sites was high and even higher if the loans were small. In the MFI model, interest on loans covers administrative costs, resulting in higher rates where there is low volume and small loans.

But the MFIs had done such a great job in bringing micro-credit to millions of micro-entrepreneurs, previously excluded from financial services that, despite the warnings, MFIs were assumed to be the ones to reach the last marginalized segment of society. Warnings from Mexico about the high interest that would be charged due to the high overhead incurred by MFIs delivering service to remote areas went unheeded.

When I visited Yumbe in 2022, I repeatedly heard that MFIs charged usurious rates and employed predatory collection practices that caused some borrowers to run away from home. They told me that with an MFI loan, they felt they were working for the MFI rather than their families. Even MFIs with excellent international reputations and the best intentions could not meet the microloan needs of small, remote communities in a way that was not viewed as predatory.

Importance of Working Through Grassroots Organizations

Like DFN in Nepal, TCP Global works through organizations already functioning effectively in small communities. These organizations tend to employ local people and do not need big salaries to entice employees to work in rural areas. On the contrary, employees are grateful for employment that enables them to remain in their community. Such organizations do not have transportation costs because they are already there. Equally important, their knowledge of the community helps them make sound decisions on loan applications, which contributes to an excellent repayment rate.

Based on their track records, we can be relatively certain that profit is not their primary motivation. Nobel Laureate Muhammad Yunus reminded attendees at the Microcredit Summits that "When you mix the profit motive and the service motive, service usually loses out." The way to benefit a marginalized community is to make sure that service is always the top priority, and one way to ensure that happens is to have people from the community run the program.

We hear a lot about the importance of "local buy-in," which is more readily achieved when the locals run the programs as in the DFN and TCP Global models. The more flexible the model, the better it is suited to meet local needs. DFN and TCP Global provide guidelines and objectives which the local leaders adapt to incorporate community strengths and address special community challenges.

Building on what already exists in a community is a good way to ensure local buy-in. This is more feasible for small organizations with flexibility. Thanks to its adaptable model, as of 2022, TCP Global works with over 70 Village Savings and Loan Associations (VSLAs). These VSLAs are typically groups of 30 women who combine their weekly or monthly savings to make loans to each other. VSLAs have been so successful that 20 years after CARE stopped training people to establish and run VSLAs, the number of VSLAs has increased.

The model is so simple that the original groups trained by CARE were able to train new groups in nearby villages. There are more than 67,000 VSLAs worldwide, primarily in small and remote areas where people have a strong sense of community. TCP Global partners in Niger, Uganda, Sierra Leone, and other African countries report that many VSLA members see the value of affordable loans and would like larger and more frequent loans than their small savings can support. TCP Global funds help them expand their loan pools to meet that need.

VSLAs in Small Villages Eager for Loan Funds

TCP Global seeks to increase its partnerships with VSLAs to maximize service to small communities. Since many of these groups lack international banking services, and computer and internet capabilities, TCP Global often works through a local nonprofit that serves as a fiscal agent for the VSLAs.

Providing the entrepreneurial poor with access to small amounts of affordable capital is part of the solution to making small and remote communities viable. Entrepreneurs tend to be creative risk-takers and change-makers. By empowering them to improve their businesses and escape abject poverty, we create an opportunity for them to go on to improve their communities, as well. The best solutions are local solutions, and who better to find those solutions than entrepreneurs? While some problems may be addressed at a household level, others, like sanitation, access to water, and malaria eradication, require a concerted community effort. Entrepreneurs are well suited to lead the effort.

Infrastructure Needed in Small Communities

Improved solar technology and internet connectivity also increase opportunities[23] in remote areas, allowing people to live a full life in their community of birth if they choose. The Casa Colibri Clinic in Huehuetenango, Guatemala, uses telemedicine to back up local medical staff with U.S. doctors when a patient's needs exceed local abilities. Casa Colibri was the first micro-loan site we opened outside of Colombia when TCP Global evolved from The Colombia Project in 2015. Before graduating, the Casa Colibri programs invested each dollar received more than eight times, primarily supporting loans for food production and health services but also for copy services and other amenities that people in their community might otherwise have to travel considerable distances to obtain.

---

23 Electricity and the internet: two markets, one big opportunity. https://blogs.worldbank.org/digital-development/electricity-and-internet-two-markets-one-big-opportunity.

Economically empowered entrepreneurs convert commercial deserts into thriving communities where people want to live. Earnings from the microloan program funded needed improvements at the clinic as well, improving their standard of medical care.

A November 2000 study entitled Renewable Energy for Rural Schools, published by the National Renewable Energy Laboratory in Golden, Colorado, reports that an evaluation of solar technology in a rural village in Africa "... showed that the introduction of solar technology to this rural village had a decided positive impact on microeconomic development, health improvements, and school performance—each of which plays an important role in ensuring continued sustainability in rural villages."[24]

Worldwide access to the internet is not yet a reality, but the government of India is working on Prime Minister WiFi Access Network Interface (PM-WANI),[25] which would establish WIFI hotspots throughout the country. Research is underway regarding options to make the Internet more widely available.[26]

With TCP Global loans, individuals accumulate resources to install solar panels and gain access to the internet, but it is even more beneficial when governments provide widespread connectivity in rural areas.

Economic Empowerment as Foundation for Rural Development

To take full advantage as opportunities arise, people in rural communities will need funds to buy solar chargers, cell phones, computers, internet access, etc. A small amount of money opens

24 Antonio C. Jiminez, Tom Lawand, "Renewable Energy for Rural Schools," National Renewable Energy Laboratory, Golden, Colorado, November, 2000. Foreward, https://www.nrel.gov/docs/fy01osti/26222.pdf.

25 PM"_WANI Central Registry, https://pmwani.gov.in/wani

26 Roku, Fukui, Christopher Arderne, Tim Kelly, Blog, WorldBank, Nove 7, 2019. https://blogs.worldbank.org/digital-development/africas-connectivity-gap-can-map-tell-story

the door to a world of information for them and their children. Affordable credit to increase earnings is key.

There are additional challenges in Nepal, where some communities are a two-day walk from the nearest road and where the people are ostracized due to a rigid caste system. While the need in Africa is primarily for capital, the additional staff support and training funded by the Development Fund Norway (DFN) are essential in Nepal. According to information about DFN on Wikipedia, "The organization's mission is to contribute, with emphasis on long-term measures, to promoting a fairer distribution of the world's resources, supporting sustainable development and local participation aimed at promoting democracy and human rights, reducing poverty and safeguarding the environment.

In the South of Nepal, the Development Fund Norway helps small-scale farmers improve food security and implement sustainable agricultural practices, which enable them to adapt to climate change.

TCP Global Complements DFN Work

While DFN provided training and support, since they did not have a micro-loan component, it was not always possible for people to implement what they learned. The need to do so became urgent when the COVID pandemic brought migrant workers home from India, and the tourist industry collapsed. Those who sold snacks and souvenirs to tourists were suddenly without income. Migrant workers unable to make a living in Nepal before the pandemic had no choice but to return to Nepal to try again under even less favorable conditions.

Training provided by community-based organizations (CBOs) funded by DFN taught newly unemployed people to raise goats, pigs, and chickens. They taught subsistence farmers to extend the growing season by building hot houses and applying proven agriculture techniques to increase yield so that families could survive despite the loss of income from tourism and migrant work.

With TCP Global loans, they could buy farm animals and seeds and build the hothouses to apply what they had learned.

Micro-Loans, An Essential First Step

Of course, it takes more than affordable micro-loans to make small and remote communities viable, but loans are an essential first step. In most impoverished communities around the world, short-term lenders charge high interest and often leave the borrowers worse off. Small, affordable loans help families take incremental, manageable steps up the economic ladder to success.

Freed from extreme poverty, people can begin to work on other needs in their communities, which is where P2P excels. People can't perform adequately at work or school if they are sick. People who drink contaminated water inevitably get sick. With a little financial support and guidance from P2P, earnings from the TCP Global loan program can be strategically invested to improve health and quality of life, a topic addressed in other chapters of this book.

Building Capacity in Borrowers and Partners 4/21/23

In March, Rotarians worldwide attended training for new officers. 7 Yumbe Rotarians took the 12 hour bus ride to Kampala where they learned and shared and connected.

TCP Global borrowers were trained to drill wells by hand - a service for their community and income opportunity for them.

Excerpts from the TCP Global newsletter of April 21, 2023

Bosh Bosh in Liberia trains young women to earn a living by sewing. TCP Global loans enable them to start sewing businesses.

Women in Yumbe who learned to make soap during our 2022 visit now teach others. They also make soap to distribute to those in need.

Learning to make soap from fire ash.

Excerpts from the TCP Global newsletter of April 21, 2023

Women in various sites request training to make reusable sanitary pads. The pads help teenage girls to stay in school.

By helping partners write and submit grant proposals, TCP Global builds capacity. Partners establish a history of grant management that will strengthen their future requests.

Chris Roesel helped the Yumbe Rotary Club win a $10,000 grant from MPI, Malaria Partners International to test, treat, and prevent malaria in two additional villages.

Excerpts from the TCP Global newsletter of April 21, 2023

CHAPTER 3

The Path to Economic Growth, Ending Poverty, and Saving the Planet

"The world has enough for everyone's need but not enough for everyone's greed." *Mahatma Gandhi*

Naomi Klein in "This Changes Everything" and Muhammad Yunus in "A World of Three Zeros" deliver the good news that we don't need to choose between the planet's health and the well-being of its inhabitants. We do need to choose, however, between greed and sustainability.

Greed is the natural enemy of sustainability since greed prioritizes the desires of a few over the rights of many. For short-term profit, greed is willing to kill the goose that lays the golden egg. Sharing for mutual benefit is the key to both a healthy planet and a healthy economy. In terms of the planet, sustainable development implies *respect for* rather than *exploitation of* resources. We recognize that to continue to enjoy our beautiful earthly home, we must protect and preserve the planet and all its natural resources. Sustainable economic development requires respect for human resources as well.

Empowering Sustainable Improvements

Clearly, this is a macro-problem that requires the implementation of solutions at the highest levels, but the grassroots is quite capable of showing the way. This chapter focuses on one small effort that has successfully empowered marginalized people to secure a more equitable share of the economic pie. It addresses global challenges like income inequality, food insecurity, environmental preservation, and migration at the micro-level.

The two-fold mission of TCP Global for 23 years has always been:

1. Empower marginalized entrepreneurs with affordable loans in perpetuity;
2. Strengthen effective grassroots organizations by providing a steady revenue stream for their community projects.

In the first 8 years, after evolving in 2015 from The Colombia Project to TCP Global, this volunteer-run program issued over 19,000 loans worth $3.8 million to 8,500 borrowers in 200 small communities, with 70% of the loan activity occurring in just the last two years. Nearly 75% of the loans were funded by repayments on loans issued in prior years. A small amount of outside funding goes a long way since loan repayments match every donated dollar annually. Only slightly over 25% of the loans required outside funding. The program could double annually with adequate seed money over the next decade.

Thanks to affordable loans, subsistence farmers in rural communities across Nepal and throughout Africa engage in regenerative agriculture, restoring degraded soils to increase food production. Anecdotally, we learned that fewer people migrated for work to supplement the family income, and fewer young people chose to migrate permanently to big cities and foreign countries now that they had the opportunity to enjoy a good life at home with their family and friends. With the increased income realized after investing in loans to improve their small businesses, parents across Latin America, Africa, and Nepal invariably invest in educating their children. It is not that parents lack knowledge of what their families need to thrive. They simply lack the resources.

Thanks to earnings from managing the TCP Global loan program, grassroots organizations have funds to improve access to water, provide latrines, plant trees, and introduce programs to reduce environmental degradation. These grassroots partners, like the entrepreneurs they support with loans, have no shortage of viable plans. What they have in common with the clients they serve is a shortage of resources.

Fortunately, the dollar goes a long way in rural villages. In the Yumbe District of Northern Uganda, $10,000 enables a village of 100 families to significantly reduce waterborne diseases, like dysentery and diarrhea, with the installation of 100 latrines ($57) and hand-wash stations ($3), 4 wells ($770) and 25 water filters ($30) capable of providing clean water for 10 years to four families, each. With microloans to increase income for the entrepreneurs and the water, sanitation, and health programs to reduce funds spent fighting preventable diseases for all families, poor villages advance along the road to prosperity.

The 21 Village Savings and Loan Association partners in Yumbe and their fiscal agent have withdrawn over $47,000 in earnings in the last two years, funding many community improvements. Since they use their earnings, they can improve their communities in the way they choose, rather than adhering to the requirements of a granting agency in some far-off city. And since they spend their own money, they spend frugally and wisely, i.e., sustainably.

First, Do No Harm

Sustainable development comes from within the community. A critical first step involves freeing potential leaders from abject poverty so they can create a better future. Micro-loans, especially for women, play a crucial role.

That's where TCP Global comes in. Our guiding principle is: "First, do no harm." We witnessed loan programs in Colombia that forgave outstanding loans when funds for administering the program were terminated, and the infrastructure needed to sustain the program was dismantled. This sent the message to borrowers in other programs - that if they waited long enough, their loans might be forgiven. It created a significant challenge for loan programs still operating in Colombia. Even without social media, 20 years ago, information like that traveled fast.

For the first 18 years as The Colombia Project and then later as TCP Global, micro-loans primarily supported clients of nonprofits working in education and health. We were a good supplement to their efforts because clients could achieve health and education goals better when they had more income. When we evolved as TCP Global in 2015, the first country involved outside of Colombia was Guatemala. As Returned Peace Corps Volunteers often do, I had my own Peace Corps country, Colombia, on a pedestal and feared their entrepreneurial spirit would not be matched in other countries. Wrong!

Dr. Jay Eastman established the Casa Colibri Clinic after he returned from a medical mission in Huehuetenango, Guatemala, and told his wife and his Rochester Hills Minnesota Rotary Club, "We need to do more." They started with a small clinic in 2006, powered by generators, where they could host periodic medical missions. Over the years, they expanded the clinic, which is now open daily and staffed by a health professional who speaks the local dialects and can consult via telemedicine with health professionals in Detroit for difficult cases. They have a mobile clinic that delivers prenatal care to women unable to make the long walk to the clinic.[27]

Recognizing that poverty was a significant barrier to health, the Casa Colibri board signed an agreement with TCP Global to bring microloans to their clients. Through the mobile clinic, Casa Colibri managed loans in multiple villages where there were just a few borrowers. Village Health Promoters (VHP) in two larger villages served by the clinic established independent TCP Global loan programs, with Casa Colibri serving as fiscal agent. After receiving a loan, Domingo, in San Francisco Momonlac, used his increased business earnings to install a stove with proper ventilation

27 https://casacolibri.org/programs/

to protect his family from the smoke that damaged their lungs. Since it was energy-efficient, it also reduced the need to cut trees for firewood. The stove served as a model for others in the village. Loans helped residents increase egg production and raise more crops. One entrepreneur used earnings to install a water catchment system on his roof so that for much of the year, the young girls did not have to miss school to fetch water. Entrepreneurs are problem solvers. When their immediate problem is no longer daily survival, they sustainably address long-term problems.

Magdalena - From Prospective Guerrilla to Health Worker

Magdalena, the VHP who runs the microloan program in Nueva Generacion Maya, has an intriguing story. The day before I visited, she delivered her first grandchild! As a young girl, she already had a guerrilla uniform and was ready to join the fight in the 36-year genocidal war when her parents got wind and nixed her plans. In a fascinating career shift you would be unlikely to see in a U.S. suburb, she decided that if she could not help people by being a guerrilla, she would become a healthcare worker instead. In her generation, girls' education was not a priority, so she learned health care by serving as a translator, assisting Spanish-speaking doctors to treat Guatemalans who spoke a local language.

When I met Magdalena, she provided first-line health care for a village of roughly 2,000 people. She was concerned about her inability to provide the full range of prenatal screenings because there was no place for women to collect a urine sample. The only nearby outhouse was down a steep path, too dangerous for pregnant women to navigate, so Magdalena used TCP Global interest earnings to build an accessible outhouse.

Magdalena understood that increased income allowed families to eat better and protect their health. She realized that adding a small micro-loan program reinforced her work as a Village Health Promoter and provided funds for clinic improvements. Over the years, Magdalena issued 177 loans with a 99.95% repayment rate.

Magdalena and Domingo set up their own loan application and screening processes and set the terms of the loans and the interest rates. They accepted the payments, reinvested those funds in new loans, and sent reports to TCP Global, sometimes by WhatsApp. TCP Global sent them additional funds based on their positive results. They operated autonomously so that if TCP Global ceased to exist at any point, Magdalena's and Domingo's programs could continue uninterrupted by recycling the funds they already had on hand. It is important to have an exit strategy. For TCP Global, it is simple: Make the programs sustainable from the start so that they can continue without our outside support at any point.

What Sets TCP Global Apart From Other Micro-Loan Programs

There is a major difference between TCP Global and other micro-loan entities. Our funds are equivalent to a grant to a community to set up a sustainable loan program. Once TCP Global funds enter a community, they stay in the community, either recycled as loans or funding community projects. Since Casa Colibri served as fiscal agent, they also received earnings, which they used for clinic repairs.

The key to success is finding nonprofits like Casa Colibri and their VHPs already working effectively at the grassroots level in marginalized communities. The advantage of this approach is that any funds needed for salary, rent, and other overhead are already covered, so there is no cost associated with starting a small loan program. Since Casa Colibri, Domingo and Magdalena were community members, they had the local awareness necessary to make good loan decisions, and their fellow villagers were likely to make every effort to repay loans issued by their VHPs.

TCP Global is built on trust, relying on recommendations from trusted sources. Dave Snyder, a Returned Peace Corps Volunteer (RPCV), Rotarian and member of the TCP Global team, recommended Casa Colibri after participating as a translator on several medical missions. Dave recommended Casa Colibri, which in turn recommended Domingo and Magdalena, who selected people they trusted to use loan funds well and repay them.

We trust, but we also verify. At our personal expense, representatives of TCP Global have conducted due diligence visits to an estimated 25% of our sites. By tracking each loan through our reporting system, we were able to alert the St. Vincent DePaul nun administering one of the programs that her hired *helper* was apparently *helping herself* to some of the payments. She would record the payment in the borrower's file, so the borrower record was correct, but then fail to put the money in the cash box and omit the payment from the report so that the money in the cash box would correctly match the balance reflected on the reporting log. It was only when those borrowers took out new loans, and we showed Sister Ruby the reported payments to check against the client files, that she was able to detect and stop the petty theft.

While the loan program can operate anywhere, it is best suited for communities like Nueva Generacion Maya and San Francisco Momonlac, where people know each other, and micro-entrepreneurs have no other affordable loan options.

Peace Corps Connections to Underserved Communities

Initially, finding good partners was challenging. Returned Peace Corps Volunteers (RPCVs) with ties to small communities were our major source of referrals. By 2021, with 70 partners successfully administering more than 150 loan sites, word-of-mouth generated an endless stream of excellent new partners. To control demand for new programs, as of 2021, we require new sites to provide the first $1,500 of their loan pool. This has slowed growth to a more manageable level and helps us screen for committed partners.

The very design of the TCP Global model attracts ideal partners. We want partners already working selflessly and effectively in marginalized communities, those willing to go the extra mile for their community. In the early days, when prospective partners learned we would not pay them anything to run the program, many quickly disappeared. The ones who remained interested were willing to take on an additional task if it meant greater opportunity for their clients. Those are the partners we want.

On the other hand, we do not want them to burn out. While we pay them nothing upfront for their good *intentions*, we give partners the opportunity to establish a steady funding stream based on their good r*esults*. Partners can use their earnings for whatever they choose, and we assumed this might include extra staff or enhanced salaries. We quickly learned that our partners are primarily motivated by the "social paycheck," with the opportunity to do more good in their communities.

Given the types of partners we attract, from the beginning, it has been difficult to get them to take out their earnings. They are entitled to take out 50% of the funds sent AFTER they have been invested twice, but they would weigh their needs against the needs of the next few people awaiting loans and delay their own gratification. Now, we have a clearly established formula regarding qualifying for expansion funds and are more proactive in encouraging the use of earnings.

Use of Program Earnings

A few partners excel at strategically investing their earnings. SONCOL in La Victoria, Colombia, is part of the MINICOL network that provides education and mentoring for children from impoverished households. The first time I visited their program, I was taken aback that they appeared to be serving affluent children. When I later saw the dirt-floor shacks where some of the children lived, I understood the profound effect SONCOL had on their lives and how TCP Global program earnings contributed to that profound effect.

In 12 years, SONCOL used more than 85% of its $32,600 earnings. When COVID struck, they had funds readily available to provide relief in the way they determined would best meet the needs of their community, without the delays and extra work required in applying for outside funding through a grant process. SONCOL also set up a sewing cooperative that produced sufficient revenue to pay utilities at their community center. Other funds were used for emergency repairs following weather-related damages to their community center.

This education-oriented non-profit had long sought funds to allow its scholars to continue studies beyond secondary school. TCP Global helped them find a way. They used some of their earnings to set up a separate loan program for university or trade school students. A little goes a long way in small communities, and when people spend their own funds, they spend wisely.

TCP Global earnings are structured to encourage sustainability. For individual sites, the main source of earnings in the first two years is TCP Global's unique 50% incentive option (Loan sites with good repayment records are allowed to withdraw up to 50% of previously received funds after they have been loaned out, repaid and loaned out again.). Those first two years are when the learning curve is steepest, and most sites receive their full $9,000 in funding, thus earning $4,500 over two years. Once they have full funding, with $4,500 in the permanent loan pool, interest on loans generates roughly the same level of earnings, given that funds are generally loaned out twice per year. In many non-profits, enthusiasm for new tasks tends to decrease with time. For a non-profit with no other steady revenue source, interest earnings keep the enthusiasm level high and the program going.

2020 Adaptation to Work with VSLAs

In early 2020, we adapted our model to allow fiscal agents to connect us to Women's Village Savings and Loan Associations (VSLAs). There are over 67,000 VSLAs worldwide, typically comprising 30 women who combine their weekly savings and make small loans to their members. In the Yumbe District of Northern Uganda, we started with two VSLAs, whose members wanted bigger and more frequent loans than their small savings could support. Care Community Education Centre (CCEDUC), recommended by a Ugandan medical doctor and screened by an RPCV, became the fiscal agent.

Within three years, we had more than 70 VSLA partners through three fiscal agents in Niger and Uganda and an additional 10 VSLA partners formally registered as NGOs, requiring no fiscal agent. VSLAs make ideal partners since they have experience managing a loan program. By joining TCP Global, they continue what they are already doing, but with more funds. All they need is a fiscal agent with a bank account to receive TCP Global funds and to file reports via the Internet.

While the VSLAs are the official loan partner, we needed to adjust the compensation formula to compensate the fiscal agent for their support role. CCEDUC in Northern Uganda is highly motivated to help the community, but making 15-kilometer bicycle trips to the Bidibidi refugee camp to collect loan data will dampen anyone's enthusiasm. By allocating CCEDUC 50% of earnings, CCEDUC was able to purchase a motorcycle, implement community projects, and hire someone to help copy and transmit the loan information for 30 VSLAs each month. For a program to work well, all stakeholders must have something to gain from the success of the program. The borrowers, of course, have affordable loans. In our adaptation of the model, the VSLA groups collect their interest earnings, but the fiscal agent gets the 50% earnings.

TCP Global Loans as First Step on the Ladder Out of Poverty

One important aspect of the program remained a challenge until our fiscal agent partner, CCEDUC, came up with a partial solution. TCP Global loans are intended to help those on the lowest rung of the economic ladder as their first step on their ascent toward greater economic security. TCP-G is not supposed to be the only step. Unfortunately, once borrowers become comfortable with the easy terms and the support from the grassroots organization, even though they need larger loans than our program can provide, they are reluctant to move on to bank loans. They relate stories of friends and family who lost their goats or land when they could not repay a bank loan. They tell of people who moved away and left their homes to escape aggressive creditors.

There are mandates in several developing countries for banks to find ways to include the poor, but the right formula is elusive. Since risk is a big consideration, TCP Global's loan history could provide a low-risk way for banks to adhere to government mandates. TCP Global recommended that the Yumbe borrowers go to the bank as a group, offer a group guarantee for individual loans, negotiate favorable terms, share their TCP Global loan-repayment history, remind the bank of the various accounts their non-profit and/or VSLAs maintain in the bank, and find out what the bank requires, in order to offer more favorable terms. As a group, they could have power. This could be mutually beneficial for borrowers and banks.

Resistance to Working with Banks

For months, their resistance remained firm. They did not want the risk associated with bank loans. Finally, our fiscal agent partner, CCEDUC, presented a solution. CCEDUC would use its program earnings to create a permanent loan pool for larger loans.

Local solutions to local problems are typically the best solutions. In this case, CCEDUC will have a permanent revenue stream from interest earnings from that pool of funds for large loans, while the interest on the smaller loans managed by the VSLAs goes to the VSLAs. At some point, bank loans will hopefully become a viable option when the entrepreneurs are ready for loans in the $5,000 range, for which banks offer more attractive terms.

Parallels in Dead Aid

In re-reading *Dead Aid* by Zambian economist Dambisa Moyo, I was struck by the similarity between our borrowers, who cling to the status quo of easy TCP Global loans and the situation she described of African countries comfortably addicted to aid, instead of graduating to use more sustainable economic tools. Moyo's recommended solutions at the macro level are similar to what we propose for our borrowers at the micro level. She suggests they enter the bond market, for example, as a group of countries to share the risks and the benefits and negotiate more favorable terms. She recommended providing guarantees to initially open the door to new economic tools and reduce the guarantee requirements over time, as the beneficiaries demonstrate their creditworthiness.[28] Change does not come easily.

As we wait for the experts to shift focus to find better ways to empower the poor, we can study what they are doing and saying at the macro-level and perhaps identify ways to apply their research to improve financial outcomes in small communities. We can make the best use of tools currently available in a practical and sustainable way.

Although TCP Global is committed to letting local people determine how the loan program operates, there are financial constraints. When borrowers' desire for larger loans leads them to petition TCP Global for funds over and above the agreed-upon target instead of working together to petition banks for equitable terms, it is time for a reality check. TCP Global struggles to secure funds to promptly satisfy requests from qualified loan partners prepared to issue loans to those just starting the climb out of poverty. We intend to serve those without other options. It is essential that the most successful borrowers find a way to move into the formal economy, both to make room for others and to position themselves for further growth.

The Importance of Being Flexible

While we generally require monthly reports, in remote sites in Nepal, it works better for community-based-organization (CBO) workers to issue all loans at the same time to the assembled group and collect only one payment in full, in the end, with all the borrowers meeting in one place. To visit each borrower monthly or require them to visit the CBO office would create a significant hardship. Loan funds turnover more slowly in Nepal, but this is what works best for them.

What works well in one setting is not necessarily ideal for others. Each site has its unique challenges and opportunities. In a June

28 Dambisa Moyo, "Dead Aid," (New York, Farrar, Strauss & Giroux, 2009) pp 77-97

2015 conversation between Tyler Cowen of the Mercatus Center and Dr. Jeffrey Sachs of Columbia University, author of "The End of Poverty," Sachs emphasizes the importance of understanding "… that the problem that you saw over there is not the same as the problem that you're seeing here."[29] His theory of differential diagnosis dispels the idea that "one explanation fits all viewpoints." TCP Global learns from each loan site and each country, and much of what we learn is universally applicable – but not everything. We achieve the greatest good when we provide guidelines, listen carefully to people on the ground who understand the local situation far better than we do and then work collaboratively to find the best way to serve a particular community.

29 https://www.youtube.com/watch?v=w8pEgvzJ7p4 (minutes 20-25)

TCP Global provides resources.
TCP Global+ is what change-makers do with those resources.

Entrepreneurs invest in education, nutrition, health and well-being.

Grassroots partner earnings improve communities.

Sawyer Water Filter ladies are trained to share clean water with 3 other families.

This makes clean water affordable and available for many more people.

TCP Global Newsletter - December 15, 2022

TCP Global Newsletter – December 15, 2022

TCP Global borrowers in the Yumbe Rotary Club live the motto on their shirts: "***Caring for Humanity.***"

TCP Global + P2P make affordable and sustainable health and sanitation improvements available to partners and entrepreneurs.

Sawyer Water Filter ladies are trained to share clean water with 3 other families.

This makes clean water affordable and available for many more people.

TCP Global Newsletter – December 15, 2022

> Poverty is the absence of all human rights. The frustrations, hostility and anger generated by abject poverty cannot sustain peace in any society.
>
> **Muhammad Yunus**

Zakari Hassane (left) of Potentiel Terre brought TCP Global loans to 10 villages in post conflict areas of Niger.

Six more villages in a conflict-prone area are waiting to join.

100% of Yumbe borrowers were displaced by conflict at some point in their lives, including over 250 Sudanese in the BidiBidi Refugee Camp. Those with raised hands are also widows.

TCP Global Newsletter – December 15, 2022

CHAPTER 4

FACTORS INHERENT IN PROGRAM SUCCESS

> "A leader is best when people barely know he exists, when his work is done, his aim fulfilled, people will say: we did it ourselves."
> *Lao Tzu, ancient Chinese Taoist philosopher*

Self-indulgence threatens organizations just as it does people. They start out to do good and stay to do well - for themselves. They may start with a sincere mission to help a worthy group, but then their energy becomes absorbed in maintaining the organization. Rather than the organization serving the people, the people's plight is exploited in what a friend calls "poverty porn" to raise funds for the organization. A Rand Corporation study cautions: "Specifically, nonprofits should determine whether or not their programmatic activities are producing the desired result (i.e., effectiveness) and whether the results are adequate in proportion to the cost of effort (i.e., efficiency).[30]

As a Peace Corps trainee, I was introduced to the "CARD," a tool to analyze the health of an organization, which made the health of the organization the top priority. This is fine in a perfect

30 Lisa M. Sontag-Padilla et al, "Financial Sustainability for Nonprofit Organizations," Rand Corporation, research Report, 2012., https://www.rand.org/content/dam/rand/pubs/research_reports/RR100/RR121/RAND_RR121.pdf,

world, where we have resources to move beyond the top priority, but in the world we live in, just keeping the organization afloat can absorb all our time, energy and funds. If an organization no longer serves the constituency for which it was formed, then I question whether that organization should continue to exist. My cohort of Peace Corps trainees largely rebelled against the CARD, finding that it left little room for implementing an organization's mission. We need balance, and leaders of any non-profit need to question regularly whether they exist for their clients or their clients exist for them. We need to focus on why the organization was created in the first place.

Case in point: Chris Roesel of P2P found a way to deliver Sawyer Water Filters and train villagers in using those filters at one-third the cost charged by the non-profit that introduced him to the filters. This seemed a great opportunity to protect many more people from preventable water-borne diseases. The non-profit viewed it differently. For them, it was a betrayal that undercut their budget for marketing, office space, and salaries. It's about balance. When $53 of the purchase price supports the non-profit and only $27 benefits the beneficiary, and there is a way to reduce that imbalance, I believe the people's needs supersede the non-profit's budget concerns.

Too often, projects are designed to achieve goals in ways that have little to do with the best interest of the target population. Sometimes, as with the water filters, it is about covering costs instead of looking to cut costs. The community may articulate their need for a more accessible water source, to enhance learning opportunities, or to access financial services. But, those lacking these amenities may be at a disadvantage in specifying how they want to achieve their goals.

> Does the community want a high-tech, state-of-the-art electric pump well, or do they need a low-tech, hand-pump version they can easily maintain themselves?
>
> Do they need used books from donors abroad, or do they want solar panels and laptops to tap into the endless information available on the internet?

Do they want a huge infusion of cash to go from zero to 80 in 60 seconds, or is incremental growth a more easily managed path to success for them?

Do micro-entrepreneurs want a series of small, short-term loans or the large, long-term loans that are most cost-effective for lenders to provide?

Is this project truly designed to help people in need, or is this a good business model or even a good business deal for the donor?

Is this about feeding hungry people or about dumping excess products?

On May 3, 2022, a Bloomberg article reported that "Microfinance has generated returns for banks and government aid agencies—and exploited millions. ... As financiers have replaced philanthropists in the microfinance industry, consumer protection has been weakened. Taxpayer-funded development banks, which could fix the problem, are instead channeling hundreds of millions of dollars earmarked for poverty alleviation into some of the most predatory lenders."[31]

Dangers of Mixing the Profit Motive and the Service Motive

At the 2014 Microcredit Summit in Merida, Mexico, each time a banking industry representative enthusiastically assured conference attendees there was money to be made lending to the poor, Nobel Laureate Muhammad Yunus gently reminded people during his next turn at the podium that if we mix the service motive and the profit motive, service usually loses. For those described in the Bloomberg article and those who pushed the profit agenda to attendees in Merida, service to the poor was not often high on the agenda.

---

31 Gavin Finch and David Kocieniewski, Bloomberg May 3, 2022 https://www.bloomberg.com/graphics/2022-microfinance-banks-profit-off-developing-world/

Damage goes well beyond the exploitation of individuals. Predatory micro-loans have tarnished the reputation of an anti-poverty tool with the potential to empower marginalized people to lift themselves out of poverty.

We seem to have a slavish devotion to "scaling up," which makes service delivery cost-effective but may also degrade the quality of service delivered. In his book *The Road to Hell - The Ravaging Effects of Foreign Aid and International Charity*, Michael Maren presents a negative image of aid programs focused more on their survival than that of the people whose stories and photos they exploit for fundraising purposes. He exposes aid programs that foster dependency and exacerbate problems rather than eliminate or prevent them.

The Aid Industrial Complex

The root cause, similar to what Dr. Yunus sought to counter at the Merida Microcredit Summit, is the perverse conversion of aid programs to a lucrative aid industry. The very size of the largest aid programs attracts corruption, undermining good governance and resulting in poorly managed economies. Many countries that received the bulk of the billions in aid sent to Africa have slid into virtual anarchy.

In *Dead Aid,* Moyo writes: "And between 1970 and 1998, when aid flows to Africa were at their peak, poverty in Africa rose from 11% to a staggering 66%. That is roughly 600 million of Africa's billion people trapped in a quagmire of poverty – a truly shocking figure."[32]

A December 28, 2021, article entitled *How International Aid Failed Africa and Made Poverty Worse* quotes Moyo and elaborates on the persistence of the problem twelve years later:

"Over the past 60 years, billions of dollars in development aid have been transferred from rich countries to Africa. However, per capita income today is lower than it was in the 1970s, and more

32 Moyo, "Dead Aid," 47

than 50% of the population (350 million people) live on less than a dollar a day, a figure that has almost doubled in two decades.

... The background behind all this is that the aid money in Africa is used for famine relief, medical emergencies, drinking water supplies, and other basic needs, which, of course, is extremely important, but they only attack the symptoms and not the cause. ... Furthermore, part of this money sometimes serves to perpetuate and sustain totalitarian regimes in power because to get the resources to the population, it is necessary to go through them, and a large part of the resources is lost due to corruption.

What a continent like Africa needs is investment in economic fields that generate structures of sustained development. This requires education, of course, but also the promotion of entrepreneurial culture to produce employment and raise the continent's production, which is the only thing that can allow Africans to have their own homes and eat their own food in a couple of decades, without having to depend on the arrival of money from developed countries.

It has been denounced that even international aid has weakened the few local producers that exist in Africa since they send subsidized products (even free of charge) to the region, which compete directly with the products manufactured there."[33]

Aid to Africa may make us feel good, but it is not helping and seems to be hurting Africa. Something is wrong, and something must change.

A 2020 article in Forbes, entitled *Corrupt Elites Siphon Aid Money Intended For World's Poorest* concurs that there are problems with foreign aid. Referencing a study by the World Bank, Forbes reports that "As much as a sixth of foreign aid intended for the

33 Emmanuel Rincón, FEE Stories, Dec 28, 2021, https://fee.org/articles/how-international-aid-failed-africa-and-made-poverty-worse/

world's poorest countries has flowed into bank accounts in tax havens owned by elites."[34]

Whenever large sums of money are at stake, there is a risk that someone will try to divert that money into their own pockets. One of the strengths of TCP Global is that working at our small scale, usually sending $1500 at a time, we are largely immune from such challenges, and since our funds go directly to the people in a very transparent way, we have local eyes on the money, providing excellent oversight.

On my January 2022 visit to the Yumbe District in Northern Uganda, I saw dozens of aid organization signs posted along the road. On two occasions, I asked different people which programs were the most effective. On both occasions, the response was "None of them." I dismissed their replies as an attempt to flatter me by implying that there was no program as good as TCP Global in Yumbe. Still, I wondered but decided that in my nine short days in Yumbe, figuring out which aid organizations were effective was far less important than listening to the people to learn how TCP Global could be more effective.

I spent my time listening, observing, and forming relationships. Over the following year, I attended weekly Zoom meetings of the Rotary Club of Yumbe, along with Chris Roesel, Director of TCP Global Africa programs and founder of People to People (P2P). The Yumbe Rotary Club includes representatives of more than twenty Women's Village Savings and Loan Associations (VSLAs) that received loan funds from TCP Global. Every week, we learn something that helps us work better together.

The work of the Rotary Club of Yumbe validates Dr. Moyo's recommendations for economic empowerment rather than aid. She maintains that economic empowerment is the root of all development at the macro level, and we see in Yumbe that economic empowerment was the essential first step for unleashing

34 Ollie A. Williams, "Corrupt Elites Siphon Aid Money Intended for World's Poor," Forbes, February 20, 2020 https://www.forbes.com/sites/oliverwilliams1/2020/02/20/corrupt-elites-siphen-aid-money-intended-for-worlds-poorest/?sh=1a7248c31565

the potential of the Yumbe Rotarians. Three years ago, 87% of these Rotarians reported the existence of hunger in their families. That figure is now 0%, and the women are busy improving their communities.

Don't Do Something – Just Stand There! (Yes!! Sometimes It's Best to Observe)

The topic of discussion at an April 2023 Grassroots Finance Action Zoom meeting concerned the importance of *listening* over *doing* or *teaching*. The best and most sustainable results are achieved when projects come from the people. If we want to help them, we need to create a space where their voices can be heard. When outside "experts" open their mouths, the locals tend to stop talking. They may be motivated by respect for their visitor, by fear of losing funding associated with the visitor, or by an assumption that visitors from the developed world know more about solutions than they do, i.e., that they are experts – which they may well be, in Palo Alto or Cambridge or Brussels.

To know what works best in a marginalized community, however, we need to hear from the resident experts first – the people living with the problem to be solved and thinking about it day and night. A little humility helps us understand that we do not have all the answers and may not even understand the questions.

Effective collaborative projects are built on a foundation of mutual respect, in which each party recognizes the value of the contribution of others. When we view ourselves as the key to program success rather than one piece of a puzzle, we court failure.

No Cookie-Cutter Approach

Before offering any advice, it helps to understand the lay of the land. It is dangerous to assume that what works in one place will work in another. In some countries, our loan partners use bank accounts to accept payments, so people don't need to visit their offices. In Colombia, however, every deposit and every withdrawal incurs bank charges. Banks provide convenience and safety in some places but erode funds in others.

Similarly, Micro-Finance Institutions (MFIs) can cover administrative overhead and charge reasonable rates when they have the high volume that population centers provide, but as those administrative costs rise, with low-value loans in low-volume rural areas, MFIs are no longer a good option. We have witnessed the truth of the sage advice of Zambian economist Dambisa Moyo and Columbia University economist Jeffrey Sach that it is important to understand the special circumstances in each situation.

Micro-loan administration was easy and cost-effective in small Colombia towns, where borrowers could simply walk by the non-profit's office to complete loan transactions, but when I visited the program in Cartagena, I realized how different the circumstances were when the loan administrator had to travel an hour by bus to visit loan sites, incurring small charges that add up over a month. The Cartagena partner had begun under the umbrella of a sister organization in a nearby town. They needed to open a bank account to end the unexpectedly high fees that the sister organization charged. It took months of cutting through red tape just to open a bank account. We cannot even imagine the various obstacles put in the path of people and organizations in marginalized communities, but we can learn if we take the time to listen.

Adapting to New Realities

It's just good policy to prohibit loan administrators from taking out loans from the program they manage, right? Well, let's think about that. When the St. Vincent De Paul nuns closed their program in Obando, Colombia, Sister Consuelo suggested that several borrowers take over managing the program so it would not have to close. Suddenly, the good policy didn't seem so good anymore. It didn't make sense to stop giving loans to the people volunteering their time and doing all the work to keep the program going. The same later proved true in Guatemala, where Domingo and Magdalena managed the loan programs and received loans. All leaders of VSLA groups in Africa receive loans, but they manage with transparency. I am frequently reminded of the quote from Jeffrey Sachs' book *The End of Poverty,* in which he equates effective anti-poverty programs with effective medical practice. To improve the health of a person or a community, it helps to understand the big picture.

This also involves continually tweaking the program as lessons are learned. The most effective programs build flexibility to improve their model continuously.

It's also not safe to assume that others have the same tools that we have at our disposal. In Cartagena, a loan program administrator noted that the leader of an affiliated savings group never wrote anything down but always had perfect records. Upon inquiry, she learned that the woman was illiterate but memorized the transactions and had a family member record them later. To keep the funds straight, VSLAs in Yumbe collect the principal and interest payments in two piles. They can count, but many are not comfortable with addition and subtraction. When CCEDUC in Yumbe extended TCP Global micro-loans to the Bidibidi Refugee camp, the camp directors, possibly as a courtesy, invited the CCEDUC leader to attend various monthly meetings, which, to the CCEDUC leader seemed less of an invitation and more of a requirement. All the other NGO representatives arrived in their Land Rovers and Jeeps, while Innocent, the CCEDUC leader, initially made the 15-kilometer trek by bicycle until he used program earnings to buy a moto-bike.

In various Yumbe Rotary Zoom meetings, Rotarians from other parts of Uganda urge the Yumbe club to buy Rotary T-shirts for special events, attend district conferences for "only $200 per person," and participate in fund-raising activities, assuming they are as affluent as most Rotarians in Uganda. We may all be in the same storm, but we are not all in the same boat. It is wise to be sensitive to the different conditions of others.

From Dependency to Self-Sufficiency

An inevitable dilemma of organizations giving material aid is when and how to stop giving, how to wean people from dependency and help them toward self-sufficiency. This is the path we prefer in theory but not the path we typically choose on our own. Just as TCP Global and P2P struggle to help the Yumbe Rotarians become less dependent on outside funding, the Yumbe Rotarians encounter dependency issues with villages they adopt to eradicate malaria and improve water and sanitation services.

After delivering twenty-eight Sawyer Water Filters and training water ladies to maintain those filters and share them with other families, as recommended by Sawyer, the leaders of Achiba Village decided they wanted twice the number of water filters they received, which was twice the number needed. Initially, the Yumbe Rotarians were tempted by the wish to please rather than empower. It feels good to make people happy by giving them what they want.

P2P and the Rotary Club's surveys indicate that up to 40% of a family's scant income is spent on medications to treat water-related diseases. By providing clean water to fight those diseases, not only do those expenditures decrease, but the capacity to work and earn income simultaneously increases. If more families wanted filters, we suggested they use their additional income to buy them.

When faced with the choice of giving Achiba more filters than they needed or providing the next village with clean water filters, Yumbe Rotarians chose the latter. Chris Roesel of P2P used a family analogy to make a point, suggesting that the Rotarians view themselves as ready to help their sisters in any village to become self-sufficient rather than as parents, ready to make any sacrifice to help their child/village. As improvements are realized in the adopted villages and the villagers have more available resources, we encourage the Rotarians to empower the villages to do more on their own.

When borrowers later requested funds for additional water wells, the Yumbe Rotarians applied the previous lesson on the value of self-sufficiency. They quickly suggested using a TCP Global loan to finance a low-tech, low-cost well available for $770 and then charging others for use of the well so that they could pay back the loan. This empowered the women and created the possibility of unlimited wells.

Buy-In from All Stakeholders

The best solutions, sustainable solutions, require buy-in from all stakeholders. If we want to stem the flow of economic migration to urban areas by improving the quality of life in small and remote communities, it is critical to get it right by incorporating the needs, wishes, and voices of local stakeholders. It is a process. It involves a "give and take" approach. It means putting local people in charge but helping them learn the lessons that will improve their chances of success. We recognize we cannot develop others because development is an individual and societal change process. The people we are working with need to make decisions, learn, build better systems, and improve. Our role is to help them gain access to any resources they lack.

This means listening, working out solutions together, respecting the people on the ground, and supporting them. It means placing the community's best interest above quotas and international NGO performance measures. We are fortunate in Yumbe to work with a united community of Rotarians, VSLA members and a fiscal-agent non-profit, cooperating closely with the district government and health entities with support from the woman representative to Parliament. This work would be difficult, if not impossible, in a fractured community.

Measuring Progress Toward Goals

It also means setting realistic goals and measuring progress toward those goals. We achieve what we measure, and sometimes we measure the wrong things.

When I worked in Customer Service at Water and Sewer in Miami, one of the measures on the employee evaluation forms was the number of calls handled. Mr. Outstanding always topped that list. The problem was that he rarely resolved the customer's problem. People don't call and wait on hold for thirty minutes to ask a simple question that can be resolved in the short time he allotted his callers. He would usually tell people to check one more thing and call back. It is not always easy to design measurements that truly measure desired outcomes.

What and Why We Measure

First, we should be clear about what we are measuring and why. Are we measuring the work effort or the effectiveness of that work? If we are not measuring outcomes, we probably need to reconsider. Outcomes are often more difficult to track than outputs, but that is not a valid reason not to track outcomes. We may have taught 50 people a new skill, but were they able to use it?

Our measures should also be objective (anyone making the measurement gets the same result) and internationally comparable.

From the beginning, TCP Global has measured the loan repayment rate since an entrepreneur's ability to repay the loan indicates their success. We calculate the repayment rate from reports the site administrators submit, thus requiring no additional effort on their part. The success of each site is measured by the average repayment rate on its loans and the number of times funds have been invested – information that is also calculated from the monthly reports. Measurement data is more reliable when based on information central to program operation rather than something tracked separately, requiring extra effort by site administrators. TCP Global tries to respect the site administrators' time, especially since the loan program is extra work they have taken on.

However, we miss qualitative measures for the impact on the families' lives. When Chris Roesel joined the TCP Global team as Program Director for Africa in 2020, he brought expertise in efficiently gathering qualitative data. Baseline and periodic random sample surveys of instances of hunger in the family, improvement in living arrangements, number of meals each day, access to sanitation facilities, etc., document the improvements in quality of life that result directly from increased earnings, thanks to the investment of micro-loans.

Such surveys only became practical once TCP Global had fiscal-agent partners like CCEDUC in Uganda and Potentiel Terre in Niger, each growing to forty sites within the first three years. Training one site leader to conduct random surveys at CCEDUC and Potentiel Terre sites made far more sense than coordinating those surveys with forty site administrators, for whom our program was a small part of their workload.

It is important to test measurement tools before implementing them widely and ensure that everyone administering the survey tool understands them the same way. We view the world through our own filters, which may affect how we understand the questions. A good way to begin is to have those administering the survey test it on each other in an attempt to identify and account for differences before going into the field. "How much your income has increased in the last six months" may be reported back in terms of an hourly wage increase, weekly take home pay or the difference between the last six months and the previous six months. It needs to be clear if we are talking about household income or the contribution of that one person who received the loan.

Furthermore, memories are not reliable over longer time periods.[35] The memory of yesterday is fairly good. Two weeks is relatively good. Longer than that is not. Also, a market vendor may report the difference in sales without subtracting the increased inventory value. The Peter principle applies here. Whatever can go wrong will go wrong. Design your questions carefully. If possible, build in a few cross-checks so that the answers in question "x" can validate or disqualify the answers in question "y" or help you identify and eliminate respondents whose information is questionable.

35 Harvard University, The Derek Bok Center for Teaching and Learnings, "How Memory Works," Time, https://bokcenter.harvard.edu/how-memory-works.

Sample Survey

To test the efficacy of water, sanitation, and health interventions, as well as the impact of micro-loans, we included the following questions in the baseline and follow-up surveys in the Yumbe District of Northern Uganda:

1. How much did your family spend on medicine last week?
2. Does your family have enough food to avoid hunger?
3. Did your youngest child have diarrhea (more than three stools per day) in the last two weeks?
4. Did your spouse/partner hit you in the last week?
5. How much do you save each week?
6. What are your weekly earnings?
7. How much was your last loan?
8. What are your weekly profits?
9. How much do you have invested in your business?

Responses to the first four questions seemed reliable. Answers to questions involving calculations proved less reliable. Some people with small investments in their business had huge profits, while others with large amounts invested said they had minimal profits and earnings. In some cases, the reported amount of their last loan differed from the loan information on file.

Tracking Impact Rather Than Effort

Even if this line of questioning is improved to elicit accurate information, it still does not track the impact of the program on people's lives as well as the following line of questioning does:

1. Within the previous (year, six months), have you improved your place of living (new roof, more solid structure, etc.)?
2. Have you purchased land?
3. Has your family improved the sleeping arrangements for any of your members?

4. Have you hired anyone to help in your business?
5. Have you improved your access to water?

One obvious line of questioning omitted here involves children's education. When asked how they used the additional earnings after investing their micro-loan to improve their business, every Yumbe entrepreneur responded that they provided adequate food for the families and paid school fees. While it was easy to continue asking if anyone in the family had experienced hunger in the last week, getting accurate information on education required a series of questions. We had to ask first if there were children of school age in the home before determining if the response applied to all or just some children. It seemed a poor use of survey time to measure investment in education when it was already clear everyone invested in it. Measures should take into consideration the population to be surveyed. Had we interviewed people who were not entrepreneurs, the questions would likely have been different.

Poverty Probability Index - PPI

One useful guide in designing measurement tools for programs in marginalized areas is the Poverty Probability Index (PPI®),[36] a poverty measurement tool for organizations and businesses with a mission to serve the poor. The answers to ten simple questions determine the likelihood of the household living below the poverty line. PPI questions vary by country and ask questions such as:

1. What is the level of education attained by the head of the household?
2. Of what material is the roof of the residence made?
3. Does the household own a motorbike or car?

Mission Statement as Guide

An organization's mission statement identifies what outcomes are important and, therefore, what should be measured and improved.

36 https://www.povertyindex.org

The mission of the Peace Corps, for example, has remained the same over time:

"The mission of the Peace Corps is: "To promote world peace and friendship by fulfilling three goals to help:

1. People of interested countries in meeting their need for trained men and women.
2. Promote a better understanding of Americans on the part of the people served.
3. Promote a better understanding of other peoples on the part of Americans."

Peace Corps, a Product of the Cold War

I started writing this section thinking that the Peace Corps was measuring the wrong things by failing to track outcomes. Online Digital History clarified the matter for me:

> "The Peace Corps was a product of the Cold War. A week before the 1960 presidential election, John F. Kennedy observed that the Soviet Union had 'hundreds of men and women, scientists, physicists, teachers, engineers, doctors, and nurses … prepared to spend their lives abroad in the service of world communism.' The United States had no equivalent. Kennedy feared that the United States was in danger of losing the battle for the hearts and minds of the world's people. He believed that a 'peace corps' was the answer. 'I am convinced,' he said, 'that our men and women, dedicated to freedom, are able to be missionaries, not only for freedom and peace but to join in a worldwide struggle against poverty and disease and ignorance. … [T]oday, many believe that the Peace Corps volunteers are this country's best ambassadors."[37]

Re-reading the Peace Corps mission, I realized what I had missed all along: that the mission is largely about cold-war politics. Even Goal 1 speaks only of satisfying requests from friendly

37 University of Houston, "Digital History," 2021, https://www.digitalhistory.uh.edu/disp_textbook.cfm?smtid=2&psid=3425.

governments for trained personnel, not what those trained personnel will achieve. Although Kennedy briefly mentioned fighting poverty, disease, and ignorance, they did not make it into the mission statement. Fortunately, they are etched in the minds and hearts of volunteers. When volunteers agonize over whether or not their service has value, they measure themselves against a standard of impact on the lives of people in their communities.

Keeping the Donors Happy

The Peace Corps faces a challenge that impacts many organizations. Do we measure so we can become more effective, or do we measure so we can stay in existence, similar to the dilemma presented at the beginning of this chapter? Ideally, funders care deeply about the organization's mission they support, and what the donors want to hear aligns with what is good for the clients. But sometimes, it is a dilemma to balance the clients' interests and what is needed to ensure that the donors continue to give so that the clients will be served.

While the Peace Corps has enjoyed general support from both sides of the aisle, over the last sixty-plus years, there are occasionally legislators and entire administrations with knives drawn, waiting to at least slash the budget, if not kill the organization, even though the Peace Corps is less than 0.01% of the U.S. government's budget. It behooves the Peace Corps to prove that its volunteers are productive and serve the best interests of the United States. It is of great service to the country, for example, that Returned Peace Corps Volunteers provide a steady stream of culturally sensitive applicants for State Department jobs and U.S.-based international corporations.

No Lobby Effort for Peace

In the country that Eisenhower warned us against, in which the military-industrial complex thrives on wars to fight and countries to rebuild, there is no counter-balancing, deep-pocketed self-interest group to lobby for funding to promote peace. As a federal agency, the Peace Corps is prohibited from lobbying. One thing it can do is justify its existence through the budgetary process.

In her 2020 budget justification to Congress, Peace Corps Director Jody Olsen reported on Peace Corps' contributions at both the macro and micro levels:

> "The Peace Corps Volunteer experience is not easy, but it is vital to enhancing our nation's international relations in spreading goodwill to other countries. Volunteers live and work alongside the people they serve and do so with limited resources and under challenging conditions. Showing American ingenuity, they are constantly creating positive and lasting change, such as in Kosovo, where two Volunteers teamed with a woman at the forefront of beekeeping to train other women how to manage bee colonies and make it an income-generating business. Another woman in Malawi has generated enough income to provide small loans to other women in her community as a result of her Peace Corps Volunteer-led training. These are merely two of thousands of examples of how Volunteers are helping women advance economically every year. … Since its inception, the Peace Corps has helped women throughout the world advance economically and become self-sufficient members of their communities. In 2018, Volunteers met this challenge with great success, having engaged nearly 240,000 women in economic empowerment initiatives. Among them, more than 75,000 women have gained life-changing entrepreneurial skills as a result of Peace Corps training, and 155,000 women have benefited from Peace Corps-sponsored workforce development education. Volunteers also helped strengthen the financial literacy and leadership skills of more than 12,000 women worldwide through targeted instruction reaching women in more than 60 countries."[38]

There is a lot of data here to document what PCVs do, and the assumption is that the various trainings changed lives. Having served twice, in the 1960s and the 1990s, my experience is that

38 https://files.peacecorps.gov/documents/open-government/peacecorps_cbj_2020.pdf.

the Peace Corps has improved in finding meaningful work for its volunteers. I am hardly a valid sample, representing only two of more than 241,000 data points. For whatever it is worth, my observation is that it was far easier in the 1960s than in the 1990s to fill one of those slots for trained men and women but then contribute nothing of value for two years. In the 1990s, there was more planning and oversight. There is still great diversity in the motivations to join the Peace Corps, and they are not all altruistic, but once volunteers are in the field, there are more incentives to be productive. The number of volunteers in service would appear to be a more valid measure today than fifty years ago.

While alleviating poverty, as it turns out, is not a key part of the Peace Corps mission, according to information on the World Bank website, "Poverty measurement and analysis have been a key aspect of the World Bank's mission for years, as is our work to share knowledge and methods for how to measure poverty more accurately and more frequently.

By measuring poverty, we learn which poverty-reduction strategies work and which do not. Poverty measurement also helps developing countries gauge program effectiveness and guide their development strategy in a rapidly changing economic environment."[39]

World Bank's Role in Ending Poverty

Their website states, "The World Bank Group's mission is to end extreme poverty and promote shared prosperity. In order to monitor progress and understand the types of poverty reduction strategies that could work, it is important to measure poverty regularly."

According to the World Bank's most recent analysis, "The international poverty line is set at $2.15 per person per day using 2017 prices. This means that anyone living on less than $2.15 a day is in extreme poverty. About 648 million people globally were in

39 https://www.worldbank.org/en/topic/measuringpoverty last updated November, 2022.

this situation in 2019," and the situation has since been seriously exacerbated by the Covid pandemic.

While measuring poverty provides no guarantees of improvement, not measuring dooms us to supposition and failure.

On 2-26-23 the Vulega savings group in Tiji, Uganda joined TCP Global using $1500 of its own funds. Average loan = $105.

TCP GLOBAL

In July, TCP Global sent $1500 to increase Tiji's loan pool to allow larger and more frequent loans.

Borrowers at fully-funded sites significantly improve businesses with 2 loans each year averaging $235.

TCP Global Newsletter – September 7, 2023

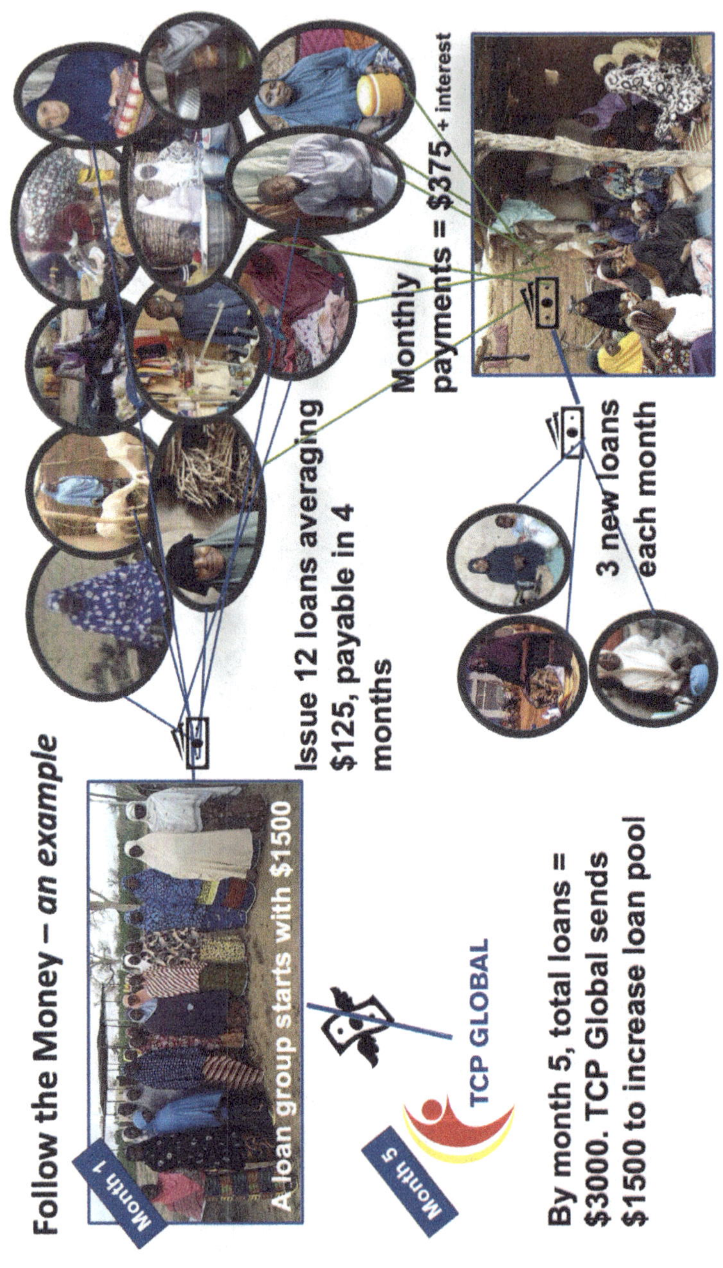

TCP Global Newsletter – September 7, 2023

CHAPTER 5

SLOW AND STEADY FOR FINANCING

> "Do your little bit of good where you are. It's those little bits of good put together that overwhelm the world."
> *Archbishop Desmond Tutu, recipient of the 1984 Nobel Peace Prize for his role in ending apartheid in South Africa*

As a Peace Corps Volunteer in Slovakia in the late 1990s, I was assigned to a newly created community foundation, Komunitna Nadacia Presov (KNP) or Presov Community Foundation, in a historic town of 90,000. The foundation's purpose was to facilitate the transition from a Communist society, in which all directives come from above, to an open society, which encourages and benefits from the creativity and initiative of its citizens. The foundation disbursed small grants to encourage community cleanups, street fairs, dental hygiene programs, historic preservation etc. It was amazingly successful, and within two years, candidates running for office found it advantageous to appear at Presov Community Foundation events. I must clarify that this amazing success had little to do with me and much to do with the young people running the program.

Several years later, KNP secured a major grant – its first significant outside funding. With their skeletal staff, they hesitated to attempt to manage both the project and the detailed grant reporting, so they concentrated on the project and contracted with an "expert" to do the grant reporting. Although they completed the project successfully, the reporting did not meet expectations, and KNP was required to return the grant funds – funds they had already spent completing the project. This resulted in the demise of the KNP.

This is an extreme case, but even successfully completed grants can cause problems.

Grants are often irresistible. They represent free money to do projects that would not otherwise get done -- funds that do not need to be repaid. But, grants may create disruptive bubbles in organizations that must scale up to manage the additional funds and then scale down when grant funds end. If one or more new positions are funded through a grant, once those employees have been integrated into the organization, it is difficult to lose those people and those positions.

Impact of Grant Funds on Spending Habits

One temptation associated with grants is the urge to take advantage of one-time funding and go for as much money as possible. It is a given that all grant funds need to be spent, even if it turns out every dollar is not needed. On an ongoing basis, however, for grassroots organizations to be sustainable, wise use of financial resources is key. Grants, on the other hand, may inadvertently encourage unsustainable behavior. The risk is greatest for young, less experienced organizations, particularly when grant funding is a significant percentage of overall funding. It takes tremendous discipline to maximize the use of grant funds, avoid falling into unsustainable spending patterns, and request only what is needed.

At the micro level, grant funds represent a tempting trap for non-profits, similar to what Dr. Moyo describes as negative aspects of aid funds to developing nations. In the KNP example and with developing countries, it is also important to stretch our abilities and develop our human resources to minimize reliance on outside experts who too often have their own agendas. We need to stretch ourselves. We are often capable of far more than we imagine. KNP could certainly have handled its own reporting better than the "expert," and nations taking aid, as Dr. Moyo insists, have resources they could develop internally.

It is not just the recipient that can lose in the grant process. In Niger, grants were given to set up recycling services that functioned only as long as grant funds were available. Since there was no real commitment to recycling, the grant recipient did not continue the program once funding stopped.

When grants are a transaction between two entities with no long-term relationship, there is no guarantee that each party's expectations will be met. Successful completion of a grant likely qualifies the recipient to apply again, but checking off all the boxes in the grant project does not necessarily mean the desired long-term improvements were achieved. When large sums of money are at stake, it is all too easy for the mission to be hijacked by greed on either side.

Strategic Use of Grant Funds

When the grant applicant is disciplined, focused on sustainability, and aware of the pitfalls, grant-funded programs can be designed to avoid problems, such as using grant funds only for one-time costs and devising ways to cover recurring costs through renewable resources. For a Coca-Cola Foundation grant request drafted for rural Niger, one-time funding for a vehicle, sustainable micro-loan pool, water filters, and wells were to be covered by the grant, while ongoing expenditures for vehicle maintenance, additional staff, and overhead were to be covered by ongoing revenue streams of the non-profit. For the long term, organizations with no guarantee of ongoing grant funding would be wise to be fiscally conservative while managing grant funds.

Incremental growth and building on what is already there is a safer path, especially for small organizations requesting grants, but large grants are more cost-effective and, thus, more desirable for granting agencies. If grant funds are necessary, as is the case in Niger, to make life-changing economic and health improvements, the question is: How do we help grassroots organizations grow to a size where they can safely manage development grants or develop their own resources to expand their services? How can they tap into the pool of development dollars at a level that will help rather than overwhelm them?

Need for Re-granting Entities

One solution is to disburse large sums of development aid to regranting entities. For example, Peace Corps Volunteers (PCVs) work with their assigned non-profits to apply for Small Project Administration (SPA)[40] grants of up to $15,000, funded by the U.S. Agency for International Development (USAID). These grants are managed by the non-profits, with participation by the PCV, and are a good learning experience to prepare for larger grants. SPA grants enable community organizations to build playgrounds, provide trails and signage for parks, restore wetlands, equip a science lab, present workshops, etc. They also provide these organizations with experience in managing grant funds. The Peace Corps manages the multiple smaller disbursements and reports back to USAID on one large grant so that all involved get what works best for them.

Grassroots Finance Action (GFA)

What is true for small, grassroots organizations is also true for individuals whose financial needs are too small to be of interest to banks. Lack of credit history and collateral also work to keep bank doors closed.

Attendees from around the world at the weekly Grassroots Finance Action (GFA) Zoom meetings led by Dr. Jeffrey Ashe of Columbia University identify opportunities for the unbanked to access financial services. There is more on this in Chapter 6, but, in short, the unbanked have developed informal savings-and-loan groups to access the capital they need to start the small businesses that help them quickly move ahead – capital that is initially not

40 https://www.peacecorps.gov/about/global-initiatives/small-project-assistance-program/

available through the formal banking sector. These savings groups, like the Village Savings and Loan Associations, are based on trust, only admitting members highly recommended by existing members.

In Nigeria, there is a variation on this theme, operating like a business where members pay a small fee to participate in a savings program that helps them become more disciplined. New members are recruited rather than recommended, and the networks may be extensive. Phone apps provide transparency to assure both the depositor and the owner of the savings program business that the middleman is not diverting their money. At Professor Ashe's weekly meetings, participants from four continents share information on best practices, such as this, for encouraging financial inclusion.

Many of the participants are former students of Professor Ashe. Many are Returned Peace Corps Volunteers. Many are Rotarians. Most work at the grassroots level, but there are a few with six-figure backgrounds running large organizations, and corporations focused on the bigger picture. All share a common interest in leveling the economic playing field. Through its network, this group has access to effective grassroots organizations serving communities in extreme poverty in the United States, Latin America, Africa, and Asia – organizations that could make excellent use of modest amounts of grant funding to provide access to clean water, small business loans, sanitation, health programs, etc. and empower their clients to make significant improvements in their lives.

One of the big picture people periodically encourages the group to capitalize on their impressive credentials, collective knowledge, and grassroots connections to help aid dollars travel that last mile to reach the poorest people in the most remote settings. Everyone likes the idea, but designing a practical implementation model is challenging. If they become a 501(c)3 to manage large allocations from major funders and then report back on the small grants they disburse to grassroots organizations, they will be creating yet another bureaucracy – requiring salaries, overhead, audits, IRS reports and other activities resulting in a diversion of time and financial resources. A more workable implementation model would involve convincing foundations to contract GFA to manage their 'last mile' fund.

Creating a Permanent Revenue Stream

While grant funds provide a shortcut to immediate funds for an organization's community projects, there is often untapped potential to develop a funding stream within the community. The TCP Global solution is to provide the grassroots organizations seed funds for a permanent loan program and a steady revenue stream of interest earnings. Each non-profit partner administering the loan program is entitled to the interest generated by the loans plus a percentage of funds successfully administered. Potentiel Terre, in Niger, is able to assure potential grantors of its ability to cover recurring expenses because they have a steady revenue stream from overseeing forty micro-loan sites. This would allow them to cover vehicle maintenance and other ongoing expenditures. Their unsuccessful grant request to the Coca-Cola Foundation was designed to avoid creating a bubble and to cover ongoing expenses.

Careful = Sustainable

An advantage of establishing a revenue stream for a non-profit to fund its projects over giving them a grant is that people tend to be careful in managing their own money. *Careful* leads to *sustainable.* In addition, the best grassroots solutions may be difficult to sell to an outside funder. We can argue that the community has 'ownership' if they submitted the grant request for a project, but this is not entirely true if they opted for what the donor would support rather than what they felt was best. When they have their own funds, they can implement what they determine to be the best solution, and they can learn and build capacity.

The lead time on grants can also be problematic, with applications submitted more than six months before funds are released. A lot can change in six months for a small organization, including the availability of the people required to implement a project. When using their own funds, non-profits have the flexibility to adapt to changing situations.

Grants can cause mission drift if an organization deviates from program goals to qualify for grant funds, shifting from what has been identified as the needs of the community to what satisfies the criteria put forth by the grantor. The Niger recycling grants appear to be an extreme example of that problem since the projects were ended as soon as the grant allowed, suggesting that the grantee had no real commitment to the waste-management program and was only interested in securing the grant funds.

There is no easy solution to the grant dilemma since grant funds help cover unmet needs, like a vehicle that would have enabled Potentiel Terre to provide support at forty sites around the country. But, grant funds need to be distributed in amounts that do not overwhelm the grantee and must be used strategically. For grant funds to be truly helpful to a developing community, those grant funds must solve a problem and reduce the need for further grant assistance rather than create dependence. What would help is a bridge to connect the donors with vast resources to non-profits with modest needs, an intermediary, such as GFA, to ensure that they both get what they need to optimize their impacts.

Need For a Permanent Revenue

An opportunity is often missed in the grant process to use a grant project to generate a permanent revenue stream for additional community improvements. People tend to value what they pay for. Instead of simply installing wells to give to a community, why not ask the community to make a sustainability plan to ensure both adequate funds for repairs and additional funds to complete more community projects, like water filters, to make water not only available but clean and safe?

Even though communities typically contribute something to grant projects, it is still worthwhile to consider how the project can yield additional beneficial long-term results. If each family that used the well paid a small monthly stipend, funds would be accumulated for well repair and additional community projects. Instead of donating free clothes, consider setting up a community resale shop. Consider a small charge for clinic visits. The Casa Colibri clinic in the remote hills of Huehuetenango, Guatemala, provides services for free, which is generous on their part, but prevents their clinic from becoming self-sustaining and discourages any other health-care programs that might consider serving the area.

We started The Colombia Project in 2000 with the idea that we should not charge interest on loans to the poor. Micro-entrepreneurs in Popayan, Colombia, told us that, as business people, they expected to pay interest, just like other business people. They were not asking for charity and were willing to pay to get what they needed.

While there are exceptions, I believe most people recognize the importance of long-term progress as opposed to short-term gains. Development organizations devoted to grassroots empowerment could help by using grant funds to incentivize the development of sustainable revenue streams to minimize dependence on outside funding.

Aid and Grants as a Small Percentage of Total Funding

Much of what Dr. Moyo writes about large aid programs in *Dead Aid* also applies to small grant projects. She distinguishes between helpful aid projects delivering sums of money equal to no more than 3% of the recipient nation's GDP as opposed to harmful projects that overwhelm the national economy with sums of cash they cannot manage well, often leaving the nation worse off. On a micro-scale, this is what happened to KNP in Presov.

Moyo also distinguishes between aid projects providing food or goods and services and aid projects promoting economic growth. The former foster dependence, while the latter empower independence. This is also applicable to smaller-scale grants. Too frequently, feel-good relief projects depress economic growth, with the result, as Moyo reports in her book, that "... between 1970 and 1998, when aid flows to Africa were at their peak, poverty in Africa rose from 11% to a staggering 66%."[41]

41 Moyo, "Dead Aid," 47

The long-term negative impact of aid in poor communities is sometimes catastrophic. Relief programs that donate tons of free food inadvertently depress the market for locally grown produce and drive subsistence farmers off the land, resulting in a long-term reduction in food availability. Another example Moyo uses is of the mosquito net business that employed ten people until 100,000 mosquito nets donated through the efforts of a well-meaning Hollywood celebrity flooded the market and drove the local mosquito net producer out of business. Five years later, when the donated nets wore out and needed replacement, there was no longer a local provider.[42]

Shift in Aid Strategy in the 1970s

In the 1970s, at the same time that Moyo reported a dramatic increase in extreme poverty in Africa, U.S. aid began to incorporate more requirements to support U.S. businesses, distributing U.S. products transported by U.S. carriers. While protecting U.S. jobs and empowering U.S. businesses serve our short-term national interests, this approach often impedes rather than promotes economic growth in the country the aid is supposed to help. As Dr. Yunus noted at the Micro-Credit Summits, when we mix the service motive and profit motive, service usually loses out. But *usually* doesn't have to be *always*.

What if contracts for aid program supplies preferred companies that committed to utilizing a percentage of local resources, or in addition to providing *gizmos*, the company would transfer technology or skills needed to help the recipient country produce its own *gizmos*? There are those who argue for dismantling the entire aid system, and they may be right, but I prefer we explore ways to improve the current system incrementally.

Aid Impact on Local Businesses

A well-designed aid program would first buy up all the locally produced mosquito nets, food items, or whatever, and distribute

---

42 Moyo, "Dead Aid," 44

those along with items donated from abroad and possibly provide funds to keep local businesses afloat until demand returned.

Food aid is particularly frustrating as proposals to improve efficiency and effectiveness are often blocked or watered down by interest groups. "Some desire for reform grew from the U.S. military's experience in Afghanistan, where USAID distributed better-quality seed that improved wheat yields, so much so that the local market became glutted. The U.S. lacked the flexibility to buy locally produced wheat, prop up prices, and distribute it to people in need."[43] The potential to economically empower Afghan farmers was missed, but the problem caught the attention of two American presidents.

Both Presidents George W. Bush and Barack Obama pushed for changes to the Farm Aid bill to provide for local and regional procurement (LRP) to allow a percentage of U.S. food-aid dollars to be spent on foods purchased within or close to the recipient country. It took more than seven years for legislation to pass, despite projections that this change would get food aid to where it was needed eleven to fourteen weeks faster and save 25% - 50% of costs, allowing the same amount of funds to nourish an additional 800,000 people.

"Congress established the LRP Program as a pilot program in the 2008 farm bill (P.L. 110-246). The provision authorized pilot projects to provide locally and regionally procured food to beneficiaries and directed USDA to have an independent third party conduct an evaluation of all pilot projects. The provision provided $60 million in mandatory funding over four years to finance the pilot projects and evaluation. The 2014 farm bill permanently authorized the program and authorized discretionary funding of $80 million annually for FY2014-FY2018."[44]

---

43 BOYCE THOMPSON, "Farm Lobbyists Spar Over Change to Food Aid," *FARM JOURNAL/* Ag W, December 27, 2013. https://www.agweb.com/news/policy/farm-lobbyists-spar-over-change-food-aid.

44 2014 FARM Bill, P.L. 113-79, https://www.congress.gov/bill/113th-congress/house-bill/2642.

This legislation was passed after Moyo's *Dead Aid* was written and is consistent with her recommendations that aid programs promote economic growth within the country. In buying locally, U.S. food aid nourishes both people and the economy.

Profit Motive Diverting Program Goals

Good intentions underlying aid and grant programs can be compromised by those motivated by profit. As Grants Administrator at the Port of Miami, I participated in conference calls outlining the process to apply for Port Security grants after the September 11 attacks. On one call, I was alarmed to learn that there was a representative of one major defense contractor in the room, which seemed unnecessary since there were very experienced and knowledgeable government employees readily available for consultation and if it were necessary for defense contractors to assist us, where were the others?

At that time, there was a need for more effective and efficient cargo screening. The contractor presented a new cargo-screening technology, and we incorporated it into our next grant request. Only after the grant was approved and funded did we learn that the technology was not actually ready. The company surely knew this, and the grant-approval committee probably knew it as well but miscalculated that the "aspirational" technology would be ready in time for implementation. When the Port of Miami recognized its inability to complete the grant-funded project and subsequently rejected the grant funds, we had some explaining to do to the governor's office. This problem could have been avoided had we been briefed by government staff, who likely knew the defense contractor was pushing technology that did not yet exist. There were likely other tested and proven security systems available through other companies that had not been invited into the room where things would happen.

Profit Motive at Odds With Service Goals

I don't know why that industry representative was in the room – whether through efforts of the congressman from the company's district, or if elected officials whose campaigns were funded by the defense contractor insisted that the contractor have special access to grant applicants, or if there was a lack of faith in government employees that prompted them to seek an "expert." In any case, I believe the cautionary words of Muhammad Yunus again apply. He states that *When you mix the profit motive and the service motive, service loses out.* Similarly, when national interests are mixed with business interests, national interests may also come in second.

When it is in the best interests of faceless masses across the sea, they are not likely to fare any better than national interests. Experts are helpful and can serve a purpose, but when using experts, it is important to verify that they are serving your purpose and not a conflicting purpose of their own. When money is available, business goes for the money because that is what it is supposed to do and what its stockholders demand. The government is charged with promoting the common good. While these two paths often coincide, they are not identical. After Hurricane Andrew in 1992, for example, Dade County (now Miami-Dade) contracted with private haulers to assist with debris removal, paying them by the ton. At least one hauler was caught watering down the load before crossing the scale. As a business model, it works. As promoting the common good – not so much.

Key Differences of Businesses, Nonprofits and Government

What works for business is always worth considering in the nonprofit and governmental sectors but is not always directly applicable. The most obvious difference is that business creates winners and losers, while nonprofits and governments are on a mission to help everyone achieve their potential.

While it might be good to suppress production to drive up costs in business, that is not acceptable for a government agency providing vaccines. While it might be good business to eliminate competition, the opposite is true for any government agency responsible for providing services to the nation's people. While in business, it is often a good idea to start big to corner maximum market share before competitors get in and before consumers move on to the next shiny thing that does not work for creating sustainable improvements in lives or communities. It is better to move forward incrementally. In retrospect, that would have been better for the Presov Community Foundation. If they had first managed smaller grants, they might have felt more confident about handling the reporting on the larger grant or at least been in a position to monitor the "expert" better.

TCP Global reached multiple milestones ....

July 6, 2023

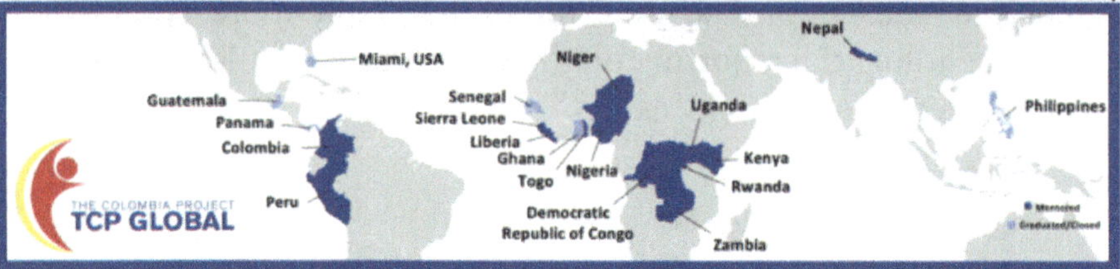

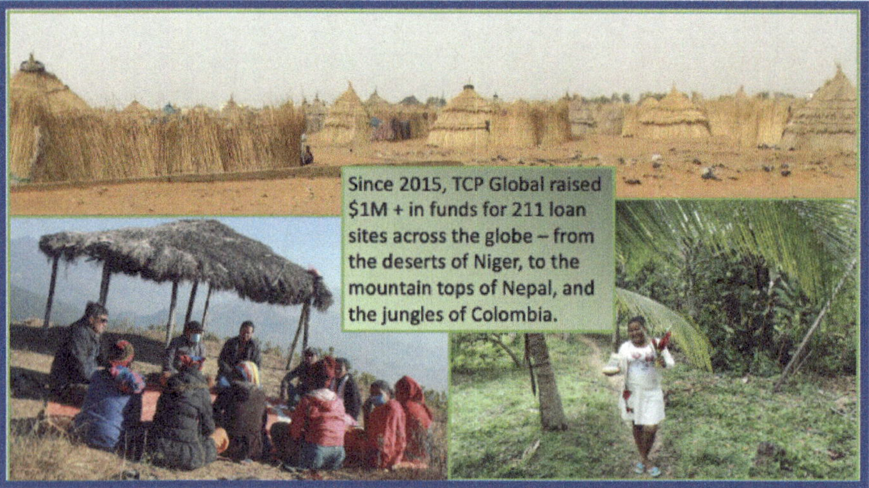

$1M raised for loans
20,000 loans issued
Value of loans = $4M+
Each dollar raised is repaid and reinvested multiple times

Groups manage their own loan funds. Here is the President of KOKARI (top), leaders of NIYAA (right) and HADINKAY (bottom) in Niger.
Worldwide, 211 groups issued more than $4.1M in loans since 2015 with a 98.8% repayment

More than 20,000 loans Issued since 2015
Average loan size $201

UGANDA MILESTONES

Programs throughout Uganda, have issued more than 5,600 loans worth $1,350,000 in the last 5 years.

$500,000 Milestone

Niger and Colombia passed the $500,000 milestone in loans issued and Nepal is very close.

CHAPTER 6

Building on Success and Strengthening the Informal Economy

> The poor themselves can create a poverty-free world. All we have to do is to free them from the chains that we have put around them!"
> *Muhammad Yunus.*

Professor Jeffrey Ashe of Columbia University leads a Thursday morning Grassroots Finance Action (GFA) Zoom discussion group "whose mission is to learn about, help shape, build to scale, and facilitate the global exchange of locally developed grassroots financial solutions."[45] He is the author of the book *In Their Own Hands: How Savings Groups Have Revolutionized Development.*

These calls are particularly valuable because they include academic research, as well as hands-on experience from around the world, allowing a sharing of best practices that work across cultures. Attendees include Returned Peace Corps Volunteers (RPCVs), Rotarians and former students and colleagues of Professor Ashe from the U.S., as well as Korea, Nepal, and Colombia, representing hundreds of years of field experience learning what truly works to improve lives on five continents. What is most interesting about the GFA approach is that rather than design programs to "help"

45 https://www.grassrootsfinanceaction.org/our-mission.

marginalized communities, they focus on understanding the informal economy already operating in these communities outside traditional banking systems and exploring opportunities to build on, strengthen, and replicate the success of the informal economy.

Best Leaders for Development Efforts

Many in the group, including Professor Ashe, started their careers in the Peace Corps, where they gained an understanding and respect for the talents and abilities of people in the developing world. It is unclear if Peace Corps service is a coincidence or the root cause of their recognition that the developing world is, at minimum, a worthy partner and potentially the best leader for development efforts.

In a March 2023 article entitled "How Immigrants and Villagers Create Their Own Financial Inclusion – What we can learn from informal economies,"[46] Jeffrey Ashe wrote,

"Three facts:

1. **419 million** adults in developing countries accumulate useful amounts of capital in savings circles that they organize and run themselves. These groups work based on commonly understood principles of disciplined savings, mutual accountability, and support honed over generations.[47]
2. There are three times as many members of savings circles as microfinance borrowers.[48] These same group savings traditions help explain how immigrant enclaves are soon teeming with new businesses and economic activity.[49]
3. The quarter billion immigrants now living in rich countries send **$529** billion in remittances to their families and communities

46 Jeffrey Ashe, "How Immigrants and Villagers Create Their Own Financial Inclusion; What we can learn." Informal economies *Impact Entrepreneur*, March 14, 2023 https://impactentrepreneur.com/how-immigrants-and-villagers-create-their-own-financial-inclusion/

47 https://www.worldbank.org/en/publication/globalfindex/Report '

48 https://fitsmallbusiness.com/microfinance-statistics/

49 https://sites.tufts.edu/journeysproject/how-to-achieve-the-american-dream-on-an-immigrants-income/

back home every year. This is three times the development assistance of all countries combined.[50]

... It is both humbling and inspiring to learn that villagers, townsfolk, and immigrants are investing hundreds of billions of dollars every year in moving their lives forward in parallel and with little reference to our efforts. What if we spent some of our resources – both technical and financial – in first understanding and then nudging their ideas along?

Invisible Informal Sector

For us living in a world of institutions, the informal sector, vast as it is, operates invisibly – there are no buildings, staff or registries, or signage – yet any villager or immigrant can tell you how it works. While our institutional world is governed by laws, the informal economy is based on trust and time-tested traditions of mutual support."

Over the years, Professor Ashe spoke with immigrant taxi drivers and hotel workers and learned that many were members of informal savings groups, usually organized within a specific immigrant population. Being part of a savings group made them more disciplined in their savings and gave them access to significant periodic payouts, which they could use strategically, such as to open a franchise business or buy a car. In 2022, Grassroots Finance Action, led by Professor Ashe, conducted

"...an experiment in Lynn [Massachusetts]. The plan was to increase the number of Guatemalan immigrants saving in 'cuchubales' (the Guatemalan term for savings circles) based on the assumption that, although many are part of these groups, others could benefit. Lynn is a small city to the North of Boston that is home to forty thousand Central American immigrants, many of them from Guatemala.

50 https://www.un.org/sw/desa/remittances-matter-8-facts-you-don%E2%80%99t-know-about-money-migrants-send-back-home

Our only instruction to the three women ... was to 'train more cuchubales."[51] They were responsible for developing their strategy, and they did."

Professor Ashe says that, to his knowledge, supporting informal savings had never been tried, so they did not know what to expect. His article continues:

"Within weeks, the three organized three new *cuchubales* with sixty-five members. In just 30 weeks, the $200 collected from each member weekly totaled more than $400,000. Each member of the thirty-member group, in turn, received a payout of $6,000, and in the two groups with 24 members, each, in turn, received $4,800. Members also contributed $30 to support grassroots development efforts in Guatemala.

The organizers reached those we hoped they would. Only one-fifth had been members of *cuchubales* before, 80% were women, and the family income of 42% was $30,000 or less, often a lot less so. Cuchubal outreach was increasing as we hoped it would. And, while most used their payouts to cancel debts and as a reserve for future expenses, those who were better off invested in a house, a business, or a car. If they couldn't make a payment, they 'did DoorDash for a few days.' There was not a single overdue payment.

When the first cycle ended, 90% signed on for the second cycle. They said that being part of the *cuchubal* had 'taught them to save.' Through their disciplined efforts, they felt they were moving forward.

With 'facts on the ground,' three Massachusetts towns expressed interest in replicating the Lynn experience. We believe the Lynn model is replicable in any immigrant community. The key is to select a local partner with deep ties in the community which can select and support local organizers who are experienced

51 Jeffrey Ashe, "How Immigrants and Villagers Create Their Own Financial Inclusion; What we can learn from informal economies." Impact Entrepreneur, March 14, 2023

group organizers. The cost is minimal. We calculate that each dollar in subsidy … leveraged $66 in new savings. …

While Guatemalans call their informal savings circles' cuchubales' Mexicans call them 'tandas,' West Africans, 'susus, Nepalis, 'dhikutis,' and Kenyans 'chamas,' every country and every region has its own name for what is the same approach. A group of trusted family members, neighbors, or coworkers agree to contribute a fixed amount, or multiples of that amount, to a common pot each week or month. Every member, in turn, receives the total collected that week or month until all have received their payout. The next cycle starts as the previous cycle ends.

In these tight-knit communities, not making a payment is 'social suicide.' Saving in small groups is in the 'air we breathe,' as one immigrant explained. Yet, if someone faces a personal calamity, the others pitch in to help. Everyone understands the rules of the game because they grew up with these groups in their home countries."

Imagine the additional opportunities to be created if the Lynn, Massachusetts, experiment was replicated widely – a missed opportunity. And savings groups are not the only way immigrant communities bolster the world economy. Remittances, another financial tool of immigrant communities, are the second pillar of the informal economy.

"Of the $529 billion in remittances that immigrants send to their family and relatives in their home towns and villages, three-quarters are used to pay for food, housing, education, and health care. The remaining $100 billion is either saved or invested in asset-building activities that generate income and jobs. What's more, half of remittances go to rural areas, where the world's poorest live and about one in nine people globally are supported by funds sent home by migrant workers. Migrants send home 15% of what they earn back home."[52]

52 https://www.un.org/sw/desa/remittances-matter-8-facts-you-don%E2%80%99t-know-about-money-migrants-send-back-home

Studies by Professor Ashe's students found that in addition to sending money home to their families, one-third of Ethiopian immigrants also invested in businesses and farms, local services, and help the destitute in their hometowns; but remittance money could be even more beneficial if more was used for development. Failure to incentivize the strategic use of remittances is another immense missed opportunity.

Potential for Funding Development

Significant development could be funded if a larger portion of that $545 billion in annual remittances supported small businesses and infrastructure. It is important to note that 60% of this money goes to rural areas, with $100 billion invested in the local economy. We need to learn a lot more about that. "While $345 million is handed out as aid in Guatemala, Guatemalans send home $11 billion. If only a small percentage of that could be better channeled, it would make a big difference."

Driving through rural Guatemala, it is easy to spot, from the main roads, which families have relatives in the U.S. They have sturdy, two-story houses that stand out from the rest, like local Taj Mahals, but those families may still live in villages that are economic deserts, lacking opportunities for the next generation of young men who will someday leave tearful mothers to travel north, to do menial work.

Imagine if some of that "Taj Mahal" money were diverted to economic development in those communities, setting up small businesses, improving water and sanitation infrastructure, and providing internet connectivity. Rather than send development funds to NGOs to deliver services with high overhead, why not reimburse expat Guatemalans for any remittances that can be verified to contribute to improved economic opportunities, such as the creation of small businesses or infrastructure upgrades?

This would put the local community in the driver's seat, determining what kind of project they want and how they want to do it, the ultimate measure of local "buy-in," with reimbursement dependent upon meeting pre-defined criteria. If there are no more affordable means of objective verification, a small portion of that $345 million of the international development fund could be used to set up a verification mechanism to approve reimbursements for immigrant remittances that fund sustainable improvements in the developing world.

The Ashe article references one informal remittance-verification process established by a group of Yemeni immigrants in Michigan.

"To ensure the money was used well, the organizers had their relatives take photos to document how the money was used. Immigrants from many countries have organized similar efforts, most notably the 'Hometown Associations' that Mexican immigrants have used for decades to support their home villages.[53]

Possibility for Better and More Sustainable Results

If we take the time to understand what good things are already happening at the informal level and then encourage and support existing leaders to expand their successful initiatives, development dollars will reach farther and create better and more sustainable results.

The Ashe article concludes: "If we start by understanding how villagers and immigrants are carrying out their own financial inclusion and add our skills to monitor progress, facilitate exchanging experiences, evaluate impact, mobilize resources, and link to other institutions, we can build on what the informal sector has achieved.

If this seems daunting, consider that all disruptive initiatives start small, but as word spreads, they can reach enough scale to have a substantial impact. What is important is starting. We will learn along the way."

I think it is important to include the work of Professor Ashe and his GFA group because they are doing what this book urges others to do: Build on what is there.

53 https://en.wikipedia.org/wiki/Hometown_association

GFA recommends:

- Find good financial practices and then facilitate replication.
- Work through established groups deeply involved in a marginalized community. They are often better at organizing savings groups than the "experts" because they are not set in their ways and are open to new ideas.
- Develop streamlined monitoring systems that collect only the necessary information to not burden grassroots staff.
- Find those who are already replicating savings groups and subsidize their efforts, especially as they reach out to poorer and more remote communities.
- Bring people together who are already working to organize more savings groups and encourage them to share ideas.
- Solicit their ideas for training more groups.
- Provide small stipends as an incentive.

"As we have seen in Lynn [Massachusetts]," writes Professor Ashe, "it may be better to start with what everyone understands. The key is to select those with a real passion for serving their community and who are eager to learn and do more together."

Following are excerpts from an Ashe Blog Post published September 8, 2022:

> "When the latest edition of the Global Findex Database arrived, I pored over the tables and graphs. I was not surprised to see that institutional financial inclusion – a bank account, a loan from a financial institution or using fintech - was growing. But this statistic caught my eye: in developing countries, while 42% of adults saved over the past year, 2.9 billion (52%) did not save at all. Without savings, the poor, and especially the poorest, face only bad choices – go hungry, take children out of school, delay urgent medical care, or turn to a family member who is probably as strapped as they are.
>
> Savings are vital for people's financial health, so these are the numbers we must pay attention to. To turn this statistic around,

we need to give more power to informal savings groups through the millions of groups that already exist and whose leaders can help to form and train new savings groups. At Grassroots Finance Action, we propose a re-envisioning of how to serve the poorest, not through financial institutions but by building on the capacity of small informal groups to direct their own development.

After two decades of promoting Savings Groups in some of the poorest villages in the world, I appreciate how savings can put food on the table or launch a business to support a family. My transformation from a microfinance believer who designed, launched and evaluated MFIs in 34 countries to informal savings advocate began in Nepal.

As the evaluator of the Women's Empowerment Program (WEP), my team and I spent weeks talking to village women about their groups, learning about how they saved, borrowed, launched community betterment projects and redistributed lending profits among the group members. A follow-up study on WEP carried out eight years after ours showed that two-thirds of these groups were still saving and lending, and the leaders of active groups had trained new ones, making up the difference. The amount they saved had quadrupled. And not a penny of external funding from financial institutions had gone to these groups.

The Nepal experience rewired my brain from credit to savings. I never looked back."[54]

Multiple Financial Tools Warranted

TCP Global participation in GFA meetings over the past year has led GFA to recognize the possibilities of a "both-and" rather than the "either-or" approach to financial options for marginalized communities. Savings groups are key to economic stability, but microloans are beneficial in very poor communities where savings groups do not provide sufficient funds to allow a small business

54 Professor Jeffrey Ashe, FinDev Gateway The Path to Financial Inclusion Must Include Saving in Small Groups Re-envisioning how to serve the poorest, building on their capacity to direct their own development, September 8, 2022

to reach its potential. Just as wealthy communities benefit from multiple financial support systems – personal and business loans, mortgages, credit cards, and insurance policies – people living in marginalized communities deserve multiple financial tools.

Savings groups are an indisputable first and essential step toward financial stability, but the entrepreneurial poor need larger and more frequent loans than many savings groups can provide. More than 100 Village Savings and Loan Associations (VSLAs) use funds from TCP Global to increase their loan pools. With larger loan pools, they can increase the size and frequency of loans so that members are able to make more significant investments in their small businesses. As the businesses grow, families have more income to invest in education, health, nutrition and quality of life.

TCP Global Has Learned from GFA

GFA has also taught TCP Global a great deal over the past year about the power of savings groups in enabling the climb out of poverty. I believe we need both affordable loans and a culture of disciplined savings, as Professor Ashe describes in the same September 8th FinDev blog post.

> "NGO-trained Savings Groups have grown into a 20-million-member movement.[55] .... These groups abound in African villages and increasingly in Asia and Latin America. 80%[56] of the group members are women. In my field experience, I have observed that Savings Groups do a better job of reaching the poorest than ROSCAs, whose members are often market vendors with a regular income. Recent research shows that savings groups save, and 80% borrow year after year, and even train new groups with little to no outside support....
>
> Informal savings groups help members to think beyond day-to-day survival as they grow their savings and form part of a supportive group that steps up in time of crisis.... The key to exponentially

55 https://www.vsla.net

56 Women's Empowerment and Savings Groups. https://seepnetwork.org/files/galleries/2019-SG-LB-Womens-Empowerment-And-SGs-EN-DIGITAL.pdf

expanding the number of the poor and poorest saving in groups is for the leaders of already established groups to train more groups.

Consider that there are a million Savings Group leaders and 20 million ROSCA leaders worldwide. Who better positioned to train and support new groups in their own and nearby communities? They understand how to organize and manage a group, they are trusted, and they live in the community and know who is reliable. Plus, they are often passionate about helping their communities.

If they received a small stipend (a dollar or two a day), they would train many more groups. This kind of incentive could motivate leaders to organize and support new groups, giving them the chance to meet with others doing the same work, exchange experiences, set objectives and help each other.

We are currently testing this methodology in Guatemala, El Salvador and Malawi, and we have found that each of those receiving a stipend will, on average, train and support five new groups per year. These "Community Champions," as we call them, are selected, trained, supported, and monitored by tested local NGOs with strong outreach into local communities.

Taking this effort to scale, we calculate that every $20 million invested in this type of initiative would translate into a million members, most of them women, organized into 50,000 groups. By saving between $0.50 and $2 per week, the groups would collectively save, lend, and distribute between $25 million and $100 million per year. Half or more would launch or grow their businesses and expand their subsistence farms. …

Informal savings groups serve those that even the most socially oriented MFI can't reach, as there is no money to be made on $100 loans and $1 saving deposits."

These are precisely the Women's Village Savings and Loan Associations that partner with TCP Global throughout Africa. They are comprised of market vendors and subsistence farmers who usually save less than one dollar per week. After one year of managing loans from their combined savings, they are eager for $100 - $300 loans available through TCP Global. With larger loans, they expand their businesses, hire workers, and improve the quality of life for their families. Professor Ashe continues:

"As financial inclusion practitioners, we need to transition from the idea that financial inclusion means borrowing (and sometimes saving) in a financial institution. If we are serious about financially including the poorest at a scale that makes a difference, our mindset must evolve from 'we have the answers' to serving as catalysts of solutions based on the good ideas of those we hope to serve – such as the informal savings circles based on traditions that go back generations. Our motto at Grassroots Finance Action is that 'They already have the answers, just ask.' Let's start asking and see what we find out...."

Building on What Already Exists in a Community

For TCP Global, building on existing strengths applies to both parts of our mission. For reasons discussed elsewhere in this book, we partner with grassroots organizations already working effectively in marginalized communities. We strengthen them by providing them with a steady revenue stream so that they can implement their vision to improve their communities. But they, in turn, work with individuals who already demonstrate both the interest and the ability to change their lives for the better – people who already have a small business they want to improve, whether that be raising chickens or goats, selling produce in the market, sewing clothes or growing corn. They are doers, and they are the people most likely to succeed.

Rather than teach a man to fish, we find the women who know how to fish, and we help them buy bait and fishing gear so they can practice their trade to earn a better living and buy extra fishing gear to teach others to fish.

If TCP Global were to help the most vulnerable, we would have long-term job security (unpaid though it is) but only incremental progress. By empowering potential leaders in the community, we achieve exponential progress, as those local leaders are better equipped than the best-intentioned outsiders to help others find the path to success, sometimes by their example and often by their own humanitarian efforts. While there are similarities, each village has unique challenges and opportunities, and those closest to the problems are best prepared to meet the challenges and take advantage of the opportunities.

No Easy Solutions

An October 2021 New York Times interview with Zambian economist Dambisa Moyo notes that there are no easy answers to complex global challenges, such as reducing poverty. This is true at the village level, as well. We tend to look for short-term, easy, one-size-fits-all solutions where none exist. When we find something that works reasonably well in one situation, we tend to apply that same solution across various settings. We need to throw away the cookie cutters.

Columbia University Professor Jeffrey Sachs often repeats an observation he reported in his book *The End of Poverty,* that the key to ending poverty is to emulate how his pediatrician wife treats ailing children, taking the time to understand the specific circumstances of each situation before prescribing a remedy. Similarly, the special circumstances of each village need to be considered in order to economically and effectively empower the village.

It is all too easy for successful people from wealthy nations to lull themselves into believing that they have the ability to fix problems of people and places mired in poverty without taking the time first to fully understand why they are mired in poverty. While there are no shortcuts, it can be helpful to observe methods that work in one discipline which may work in another. The beauty and paradox of life on our planet is in discovering how much we all have in common and how unique we are. The key is to recognize commonality and adapt to the unique situation. In Moyo's writings on macroeconomics, I see much that is adaptable to improve life in small African villages.

A guide to successful community empowerment goes far beyond recognizing differences in Latin American, African, and Asian cultures or immersing oneself in the history and culture of Zambia or Uganda. Within a country, there are also significant differences between urban and rural settings and between villages near and far from the capital. Access to water and roads and a region's history of conflict and displacement are also relevant.

While it would be a deal killer for any international aid organization to set a standard for understanding each beneficiary village or region at that level, there is another way. Finding and working with grassroots organizations already working effectively in an area checks off this requirement and opens the door to myriad possibilities:

1. A partner already working effectively in an area will likely have built a level of respect within the local community to facilitate program implementation.
2. An existing partner will already have knowledge of the community, which will make them more effective.
3. By working with and strengthening an existing grassroots organization, whatever project is implemented has a greater chance of sustainability.
4. Recruiting staff, especially for small and remote communities, can be difficult, whereas expanding and training staff of an existing organization will likely be cheaper, better, and easier.
5. With basic infrastructure (utilities, office space and equipment) already in place, start-up costs will be lower, even if that infrastructure needs expansion.
6. Community buy-in is enhanced when a grassroots organization runs the program.

Sound Strategy to Build on What Is There

Building on what is there and strengthening local institutions is a sound strategy for any development or aid program. This also requires letting locals set priorities and take the lead. If outsiders want to get involved, the best way is to empower rather than direct. Without being paternalistic, a parental perspective lends helpful insights. Just as parents want their children to grow to be independent, healthy, and happy adults, our goal in development should be to empower independent, healthy, and happy communities.

Austrian-born psychologist Bruno Bettelheim wrote: "The parent must not give in to his desire to try to create the child he would like to have, but rather help the child to develop in his own good time to the fullest, into what he wishes to be and can be, in line with his natural endowment and as the consequence of his unique life in history." The same may be said of community development.

Economist Bill Savedoff of the Inter-American Development Bank wrote in November 2015 that the Paris Declaration of Aid Effectiveness, endorsed by 92 countries in 2005, "Recognized that aid recipients are agents of their own development and called for aid programs to be structured in ways that would give them greater ownership of development goals and processes. The Paris participants recognized that when the recipient government has autonomy, it becomes responsible for the outcome."[57] I would add that we can substitute "village" for "government."

So, since this recommendation was made nearly 20 years ago, there must be great progress by now. Actually, no, because good recommendations too often go unheeded.

Hubris is part of the problem. Savedoff explains, "Despite its promise, this new aid paradigm faces strong resistance. It is easy to justify the paternalistic approach to aid by arguing that recipient countries are too weak and too fragile and have too little capacity to make progress without the direct involvement of international experts in diagnosing and solving their problems."

Paternalism intensifies as you descend the pyramid of money and power. We are far too ready to believe that those with less

57 Savedoff, William D. "A Better Model for Foreign Aid." *Current History*, November, 2015, 114(775): 316- 321.

money and power are to blame and that their deficiencies keep them down. We falsely believe that involving them in planning for a better future could impede progress. It is a convenient line of thinking that saves staff time and relieves staff of the burden of traveling outside their physical and mental comfort zones.

Treat This Program as if Your Children's Future Depended on It.

It will not be easy, but if your family lived in that village, would you take the time to get it right? I would like to see a sign in every international aid organization advising staff to "Treat this program as if your children's future depended upon it."

A friend who worked for a major international aid organization in Haiti complained of a lack of support from her supervisors for initiatives that her community needed and wanted. Since she was a considerable distance from Port-Au-Prince, central office staff rarely made it to her site.

Along with empowering local entities, aid organizations need to hire staff they can trust, empower them, and verify their work through occasional site visits. There are stories of aid organization supervisory staff who never visit sites, although they pass nearby on weekend trips to the beach.

During my Peace Corps Slovakia service, I was on the opposite end of the country from the Peace Corps headquarters in Bratislava, but my program manager visited me multiple times. That made for high-quality supervision. Since Julius, my program manager, had visited my site and met the community, I was never hesitant to consult with him when I confronted a problem because I knew he understood the situation and the people involved.

As head of TCP Global, I gained tremendous insight by visiting program sites in Uganda, Kenya, Colombia, and Guatemala, which made me far more effective in helping them build on their own success. It also helped me understand that each community has unique opportunities and challenges.

After bonding with program leaders, the chance for misunderstandings is reduced, and we are able to work through challenges and better identify opportunities. My visits increased my respect for local partners and what they do in difficult situations. Once you have personally endured transportation difficulties, watched women carefully dealing with district officials who flaunt power by exercising whimsical and tyrannical control, witnessed the wisdom and compassion of other leaders, and heard borrowers relate the life-changing impact of their loans, you approach the work with renewed zeal and hopefully, increased effectiveness. I pay my own way and work for free. We should expect no less from paid staff. There is simply no way to build on the strengths of a community if we do not take the time to know the community or delegate decision-making to someone who does.

Goals That Encourage Greater Awareness of the Local Situation

To measure community development programs, employees could establish sustainability goals for their programs and could be evaluated based on measures such as:

1. What percentage of your programs have you visited in the past year?
2. How many program beneficiaries have progressed to the level where they no longer need services and have graduated, making room for new clients? What is the percentage?
3. If you supervise field workers, how many of their sites have you visited in the last year? What percentage is that?
4. What progress have you made this year toward sustainability goals?
5. What has been your greatest challenge? Greatest accomplishment?
6. What program adjustments were made this year to incorporate community input?

7. How many capacity-strengthening, peer-to-peer learnings, and stakeholder consultations were conducted within the past year? What kinds of changes, if any, resulted?

If we visit people, get to know them, and understand their situation, we can work with them more constructively. When they call unexpectedly at 7:45 a.m. to conduct phone interviews, understanding the difficulty involved in assembling people and getting a good internet connection, you immediately seize the opportunity rather than complain that you are not prepared and that they never confirmed the appointment. Once we see what it is like to walk in their shoes, mole hills no longer become mountains.

Donating to TCP Global Addresses 4 Serious Global Challenges July 28, 2022

REDUCE EXTREME POVERTY

With an $84 loan, Balkissa bought a 25-liter can of oil and a bag of wheat flour. In the morning, she makes donuts bought by those who go to the fields. In the evening she sells to young people in her village in **Niger**.

Thanks to a loan of $208 from TCP Global partner CBODC-Sashakta in Nepal, Janu (36) invested in vegetable farming to better support her family of six. She expanded her growing seasons and diversified crops to now include bitter gourd, pea, bottle gourd, chili, tomato, cabbage, cucumber and pumpkin.

REDUCE ECONOMIC MIGRATION

Meet Niruta. She used a $215 loan plus $115 of her savings to buy 1 male and 4 female goats. She repaid her loan, sold a few goats and still has 10 with plans to add more. She is pleased her husband can stay home to help in her business rather than migrating for menial work in India. She writes she is "... very happy with the loan provided by PJBS/TCP Global and wants to thank them for the funds to support poor farmers living in remote areas in **Nepal**."

REDUCE FOOD INSECURITY

This **Sudanese** refugee in the BidiBidi camp used a $54 loan to buy a goat, a pair of ducks (which are now 10) and sow a maize and sorghum garden. Her income has increased.

She says it is fortunate she has the extra income since the world food program reduced rations for refugees. "Thank God for bring us TCP Global program"

With war in Ukraine, the World Food Program projects further reduction in food rations. TCP Global partners are working to increase food production in the camp.

With her loan, Claire bought nutritive feeds & salt licks, dewormed the cows and planted nutritional grasses Cows that barely produced enough milk for her family now yield profits that enabled Claire to buy 7 chickens. ***Kenya***

ENVIRONMENTAL PROTECTION

Borrower in Neiva, Colombia received a loan for recycling.

Partners in Uganda built latrines and cleaned Achiba Village.

Potentiel Terre in Niger provides recycling jobs for youth

Yumbe, Uganda partners planted trees.

CHAPTER 7

Economic Empowerment: Cornerstone of Sustainable Development

> "Thank you for commending our women of Yumbe district. Indeed, they have the energy and willingness to grow bigger. The best long-lasting solution of empowering these women is what you already started. Empowering them economically."
> *March 3, 2023, email from Avako Melsa, Yumbe District Member of Parliament (MP) in Uganda.*

Dr. Dambisa Moyo, described in the October 9, 2021, New York Times as "The Zambian Economist at the Crossroads of Global Business," explains why economic empowerment is important for political stability. "We can't have enormous inequality in society and expect things to be stable. I grew up in Africa. I understand that you cannot be in the one percent and think that everybody else living in poverty doesn't affect you. It does."[58] Her website proclaims: "Our ability to create and sustain economic growth is the defining challenge of our time."

While global leaders and academics work on global solutions, TCP Global makes a small contribution towards the solution by

58 David Gelles, "The Zambian Economist at the Crossroads of Global Business," New York Times, October 9, 2021 https://www.nytimes.com/2021/10/09/business/dambisa-moyo.html

empowering entrepreneurs to develop small businesses and create jobs at the grassroots level. A survey of 184 borrowers who received loans from TCP Global in Yumbe, Uganda, indicated that 39% added a total of 119 employees in 2022.

Thanks to a TCP Global loan, Rukia Driciru graduated from selling goods on a mat in a dusty street near the Yumbe market to a modest kiosk where she can secure her goods at night. She now has three employees. She can also afford to pay someone to fetch water, adding productive hours to her day. With her increased earnings, she has moved from a thatched hut where everyone slept on a grass mat on the ground to a solid house in which everyone has a bed and their own bedroom. The house construction and purchase of furnishings made a small contribution to the growth of the local economy in Yumbe. When multiplied by over 1000 TCP Global borrowers in Yumbe, there is a significant impact.

Countries and Communities Need Economic Stability

While grassroots empowerment is essential to the solution, the defining challenge of our time will not be adequately addressed by grassroots efforts alone. This systemic problem requires systemic change. In her highly regarded 2009 book *Dead Aid,* Dr. Moyo maintains that aid stunts economic growth, undermines local production, breeds corruption, and contributes to political instability. She writes, "The notion that aid can alleviate systemic poverty, and has done so, is a myth. Millions in Africa are poorer today because of aid; misery and poverty have not ended but increased. Aid has been, and continues to be, an unmitigated political, economic, and humanitarian disaster for most parts of the developing world."

Rather than aid as currently disbursed, countries need to develop economic stability. "What is clear," Dr. Moyo writes, "is that democracy is not the prerequisite for economic growth that aid proponents maintain. On the contrary, it is economic growth that is a prerequisite for democracy; and the one thing economic growth does not need is aid."[59] She maintains that aid, which is too

59 Moyo, "Dead Aid," 43

often diverted from its intended purpose, enriches the coffers of officials. With a steady flow of aid, the government does not need to be responsive to its people. In fact, officials corrupted by aid use their aid-fueled wealth to strengthen the police and military to keep themselves in power. She writes. "So, to my mind, first and foremost, how do you improve people's living standards? You've got to have growth."

Capitalism with regulation provides that growth. Clearly, it will take more than our TCP Global borrowers and their small investments in micro-enterprises, but they are part of the solution, building from the grassroots up while governments that heed Dr. Moyo's call encourage capital investment. When governments depend on tax revenue instead of aid, there is a healthy symbiotic relationship with the tax-paying public since the government needs the support of its own people to stay in power. By and large, people want to believe in their country. They want to be part of something bigger than themselves. National identity and national pride are the natural order. It was palpable on my visits to Colombia and Uganda, as well.

When governments depend on tax revenue rather than the generosity of foreign donors, conditions are ripe to decrease inequality. More earnings for everyone equals more revenue for the government. And there is a shift in government spending to things that help people rather than control their discontent – things like roads, schools, and health facilities.

"Do I think that short-termism helped create inequality?" Moyo says the answer is, "Yes, I absolutely do. If we had spent that money investing in infrastructure spent that money educating people instead of fighting wars, for example, I think we would have had a different outcome. But is capitalism inherently bad? No. I think we probably need some more regulation. We probably needed more efficient government. We didn't have those things. But I think it's a bit too easy to say, 'Oh, capitalism equals more inequality.' I don't buy that."

When I was in graduate school in the late 1980s, a professor predicted that the recent shift to short-term thinking would prove problematic. Companies were no longer judged on long-term measures but solely on the bottom line for the current quarter. That trend is reflected in society today, with our fixation on the daily rise and fall in the stock market. Government policymakers focus on short-term solutions that win votes based on ineffectual policy proposals that are readily reduced to sound bites.

While the problems and needs of the developing world differ from those of established Western democracies, the solutions proposed by Dr. Moyo and other renowned economists have relevance in both spheres. Observations by Jim Tankersley, White House correspondent for the New York Times, regarding the importance of the U.S. middle class are directly applicable to the developing world.

In a May 18, 2012 article in The Atlantic entitled *The 100% Economy: Why the U.S. Needs a Strong Middle Class to Thrive*, Jim Tankersley wrote, "For nearly all of the recorded economic past, rising national wealth went hand in hand with rising equality. A seminal 2000 study by World Bank economist William Easterly, 'The Middle-Class Consensus and Economic Development,' found that countries with larger middle classes enjoy higher levels of growth and income, along with a variety of health benefits such as lower infant mortality rates and greater life expectancy."[60] Anything we can do to increase and strengthen the middle class, whether that be in Omaha or Yumbe, will be a good thing.

The Tankersley article in The Atlantic summarizes an interview with innovator and venture capitalist Nick Hanauer. "We've had it backward for the last 30 years," Hanauer said … "Rich business people like me don't create jobs. Rather, they are a consequence of an ecosystemic feedback loop animated by middle-class consumers. When the middle class thrives, … businesses grow and hire, and owners profit."

---

60 Jim Tankersley, "Why America Needs a Strong Middle Class to Thrive." Atlantic, May 18, 2012

Ripple Effects of Enlightened Policies

The ripple effects of pursuing enlightened policies are far-reaching. In an August 16, 2020, article in The Atlantic, Tankersley writes, "Societies with a strong middle-class experience higher levels of social trust but also better educational outcomes, lower crime incidence..."[61]

While governments, international finance organizations, and think tanks sort out the big picture, effective work is going on at the grassroots level to foster economic growth and development. People are poor not because they are lazy or inept but primarily because they lack resources. The entrepreneurial poor can be relied upon to identify what they need to get ahead accurately. As we saw in the previous chapter, impoverished entrepreneurs invest in building a better future through remittances and savings groups. TCP Global loans have helped 9000 of them to the tune of $4.3 million in the last seven years.

Every borrower interviewed in Yumbe invested in education. When Virginia Emmons confronted a host of pressing needs in her new Peace Corps site, the residents of Kabey Fo asked for help with none of the immediate, short-term needs. They asked for education for their children. Communities in Niger are working to implement recycling and waste collection. Yumbe Rotarians are winning the battle against preventable diseases like dysentery, diarrhea, and malaria. They are not asking for a handout to survive today, but they would welcome our investment to help them build a more prosperous tomorrow.

With her emphasis on growth, I imagine Dr. Moyo would applaud the work of the women in Yumbe, where more than 1,000 borrowers in 34 Women's Village Savings and Loan Associations (VSLAs), have expanded their small businesses, primarily as subsistence farmers and market vendors. But they are barely the tip of the iceberg of possibilities. As of this writing, due to limited resources, TCP Global supports only 25 VSLAs in Yumbe and nine in the nearby Bidi Bidi Refugee Camp, while there are

61 Jim Tankersley, "We Killed the Middle Class. Here's How We can Revive It." Atlantic, August 16, 2020

reportedly more than 1,000 VSLAs in Yumbe District and at least another 100 in the South Sudanese refugee camp, many of which have asked to join the TCP Global program.

USAID Recommendation for VSLAs

Among the findings of an April 2019 USAID Village Savings and Loan Association Assessment conducted in southwest Uganda was the recommendation "to ensure the VSLA accrues enough capital to provide adequate loans to its members."[62] The VSLAs participating in the study called on NGOs to provide financial support toward that end, which is precisely what TCP Global does. TCP Global currently relies primarily on individual donations and could support more programs with support from a major foundation.

Borrowers report that when borrowing from the pool of combined savings of the VSLA members, they only occasionally received loans of $40, which was not enough to make a meaningful investment in their business. TCP Global loans are more than four times the size of loans issued by VSLA, and they are available twice a year, allowing the women to buy a sewing machine, hire an employee, expand inventory, increase family income and boost the local economy. Before joining the TCP Global program, 87% of borrowers, whose only source of business capital had been the small VSLA loans from their combined savings, reported periodic hunger in their homes, which disappeared within four months of their first TCP Global loan.

Entrepreneurial Poor As a Good Investment

When we put funds into the hands of the entrepreneurial poor, good things happen. First, they spend it locally – on food, clothes, concrete blocks to build homes, and metal sheets for rain-proof roofs. They pay school fees, so teachers get paid. Each step forward they make in their businesses and their homelife creates a positive ripple effect in the local economy. Contrast this with a generous

62 https://pdf.usaid.gov/pdf_docs/PA00TRWH.pdf.

contribution of food aid for a starving family supplied by farmers from abroad. One family gets relief from hunger for one day. Assuming they might otherwise have invested pennies in cassava to relieve their hunger, the vendor will have to wait another day to benefit from their purchase. If multiple families received food donations that day, the cassava vendor's family may well experience hunger that night.

The TCP Global borrowers who became Rotarians in Yumbe invest in the future. They go for long-term improvements: digging wells to provide access to water, planting trees to improve the environment and repel mosquitoes, and bringing health care to impoverished communities. In Niger, our partner Potentiel Terre is working to expand recycling and waste-collection services in two communities. They tell us that progress in improving infrastructure becomes possible once people have enough to eat and are economically empowered. When the poor move up to the middle class, they improve their communities. As the middle class expands, inequality contracts. In fact, when the middle class grows, the country as a whole enjoys greater health and prosperity.

As long as people are absorbed in fighting off hunger and struggling to meet basic human needs, they have no time or energy to improve their lives or their communities. We don't know what they will do once obstacles are removed, but we know what happens when they remain in place. Women with bright ideas for improving their children's school remain mute, feeling they have no right to speak out if they have not paid school fees. The gap between the haves and have-nots grows. The next generation does not get properly educated. Hopelessness and discontent become the breeding ground for crime, anti-government activities, and international terrorism. Society's most valuable resources, its human resources, remain untapped. We all lose, even the top one percent, for they and their children also suffer the consequences of living in a dysfunctional society. It doesn't have to be that way.

Women Leading the Fight Against Disease

June 15, 2023

Community mobilization meeting on malaria in Kuji Village in the Yumbe District of Northern Uganda. TCP Global borrowers who formed the Yumbe Rotary Club organized the effort.

First: Getting good information to share

District Malaria focal person explaining signs of malaria and preparing Rotarians to work effectively in villages.

Training of Village Health Teams (VHTs) and Rotarians on proper malaria treatment for children and adults.

District Health Officer training VHTs and Rotarians on record keeping and reporting.

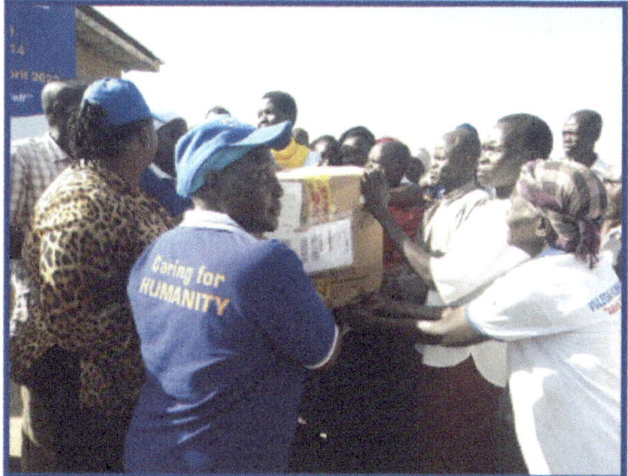

Yumbe Rotarians adopted TIJI near the Sudan border, opened a loan program, and have support of P2P to install wells and latrines and fight malaria and waterborne diseases.

Yumbe Rotarians and P2P continue trying to access some of the million+ treated nets awaiting distribution in the capital, Kampala. After a year of effort, P2P decided to run a pilot, using its own funds, to document improvements when nets are added to the Rotarians' fight against malaria.

Yumbe Rotarians trained women in Tiji to use and maintain Sawyer Water Filters which can provide clean water for 4 families for up to 10 years.

CHAPTER 8

TCP GLOBAL PLUS: UNLEASHING THE POTENTIAL OF EMPOWERED LOCAL LEADERS

"The trouble with being poor is that it takes up all your time."
Willem de Kooning, Artist

Once people satisfy their basic needs and no longer feel poor, they have the time and energy to achieve their potential. TCP Global loans enable the entrepreneurial poor to build better lives. With the TCP Global loan program, there is far more than meets the eye. That's what we call TCP Global Plus (TCPG+). For 23 years, the dual mission of The Colombia Project – TCP Global has remained the same: provide affordable loans to marginalized entrepreneurs and establish a steady revenue stream for community projects of effective grassroots organizations. We accomplish this by building sustainable micro-loan programs in marginalized communities, with 100% of our program dollars directly supporting micro-loans. That is all we fund, but that is just the tip of a giant iceberg of program results.

We anticipated that grassroots partners would use earnings of roughly $1000-$2000 per year to do community projects and, depending on what the community wanted, we would connect them to other organizations to help them address water, sanitation, hygiene, environment, health, empowerment, connectivity, and education needs.

Making Marginalized Communities Viable

People to People (P2P), an organization founded and led by Chris Roesel, a Returned Peace Corps Volunteer and member of the Rotary International cadre of Water, Sanitation and Hygiene (WASH) experts, works with multiple TCP Global partners but primarily in Yumbe District of Northern Uganda. Chris brings a wealth of knowledge and experience accumulated over his long international development career on three continents. Chris is also TCP Global's Director for Africa Programs. Our vision is to help marginalized communities become viable so that people are not forced to emigrate for economic reasons. In Yumbe, Uganda, we found extraordinary partners.

Training Local People to Drill Affordable Wells

In February 2023, Chris funded Brighton Kaniki, an expert well-driller from Malawi recommended by Henk Holtslag of Smart Centre Group,[63] to teach local people how to use the Msuzu technique to hand-drill wells at less than one-seventh the cost of traditional borehole wells. Two professional, well drillers from Yumbe participated in the training and shared what they learned with the 38 members of the Yumbe Society of Well Builders and Repairers. Six well-drillers came from towns several hours away to learn the process. Much to our surprise, seven Rotary women completed the training as well. In the following six months, they completed drilling a new 13.8 meter well, repaired two existing wells, and proceeded to drill more wells in the district, paid both by individuals and P2P Inc.

By gaining hands-on awareness of how wells are damaged and how they can be repaired, the women say they are better prepared to train villagers to maintain their wells, making these improvements

63 https://smartcentregroup.com/

sustainable. Since the women are well-drillers themselves, they can speak with authority, and people listen. The benefits are widespread. With clean and more accessible wells, fewer people will suffer from waterborne diseases, they will waste less money treating illnesses, and young girls will be able to attend school instead of spending their days fetching water.

Helpful Rotary Connections

The well project was possible because the water table in Yumbe is shallow and equally important. It was possible because a network of Rotarians supported the project. The Rotary E Club of WASH includes experts who pre-screened Yumbe for suitability. If the water table is too deep or if there is the wrong type of soil, hand-drilled wells are not feasible. Rotarian reassurance that conditions were good in Yumbe allowed the project to go ahead. Rotarians from as near as 90 kilometers and as far as the capital helped procure the pipes and other items that were not available in Yumbe. In turn, Yumbe invited Rotarians from other clubs in Uganda to participate in the training and make the more affordable technology widely available.

The Rotary women of Yumbe frequently mention how grateful they are to be connected to the rest of the world, to exchange ideas, learn from others, another benefit of TCP Global Plus. They identify the problems they want to address and how they wish to proceed. We share our experience and connect them to outside experts to help them be more effective.

An Ambitious Schedule in Yumbe

During the April 12, 2023, Rotary Club of Yumbe Zoom meeting, Chris asked if the Rotarians might have more work than they could handle. They were working on malaria eradication in eight villages and water and sanitation in three more. They had 10 youths training in Machangana, making bricks and installing latrines, and five more installing Mzuzu (hand-drilled) wells. They were also planning a huge event to launch programs funded through a Malaria Partners International grant, recognizing that every local official and district health agency would appreciate a photo op associating them with a popular community effort. This, in turn, would likely make those officials more receptive to future offers of collaboration by the Yumbe Rotary Club.

The event provides an opportunity for everyone with the potential to influence health programs in Yumbe to become familiar with the first program in their district and to do malaria treatment through a community-wide effort rather than on a case-by-case basis. Despite this long list of significant commitments, the Rotarians indicated that they had time for their current projects and could, in fact, do more. They noted that they were assisted by volunteers within the communities they served, which they said was essential for program success. They replied that it was all about good planning and making schedules and that they were certain they wanted to do more. They also kept their eyes on sustainability. In Tiji Village, each family must contribute 1,000 Uganda Shillings each month so that the village can stockpile malaria testing and treatment supplies to sell at less than one-half the cost at pharmacies. After the first round of malaria treatment is completed with grant funds, they will also be prepared to treat new outbreaks cost-effectively. P2P and TCP Global did not need to teach the Yumbe Rotarians how to plan, organize, or prioritize. We simply needed to find them resources to accomplish their dreams for their communities.

Machangana is Rotary Club President Rukia's village, and therefore, she is the lead person for this particular project. Since we always hear reports from Rukia Driciru and Lenny Christine, the first two presidents of the Rotary Club of Yumbe, I was curious to know how many other Rotarians were fully committed to these projects and was pleased to learn all 24 Rotarians are committed.

Disaffected Young Men

While it is not an official component of the "adopt-a-village" effort or the Malaria Partners International grant, the Rotarians structure these initiatives to address a problem that has concerned them for several years – the anti-social behavior of disaffected and disengaged young men. In each village where the Rotarians work, they seek to engage young men in learning to make bricks, construct latrines and dig wells and are pleased with the young men's response to the opportunity to be productive. Just as bad examples spread throughout a community, so can positive examples. As the Rotarians offer more opportunities for young men to make constructive use of their time, the women are prepared to nurture young leadership. This is not a job for them, it is not a box to check off on a grant – it is their future, and they are managing it with great wisdom and care.

What Motivates Yumbe Rotarians

The incoming secretary of the Rotary Club, Anderu Shimura, partly explained the motivation behind the Rotarians' commitment. She said people in her village no longer regard her as unimportant. Now that she knows how to drill wells, they view her with admiration, as an "engineer," and she has a Mzuzu certificate to verify her status. Rukia reinforced Anderu's comments with her own, noting that women are now viewed with respect, and people actually listen to them.

As they gain experience, their work becomes easier. As they gain success, they are motivated to do more. For example, they have already distributed more than 100 Sawyer PointOne water filters and trained people to share them with three other families to ensure safe drinking water for 10 years. With each new village, the distribution of filters becomes easier and something that can be delegated, perhaps even to young people, to do with oversight.

Improved Financial Situation for Families

In each adopted village, Rotarians work to improve the financial health of the families. Admitting one or two Village Savings and Loan Associations to the TCP Global micro-loan programs is an important first step so that the village entrepreneurs gain access to the larger loans they need to improve their businesses significantly. As we progress in increasing family incomes through micro-loans, Chris works to reduce the amount of money families spend combatting preventable illnesses, amounts that can exceed 40% of their incomes. In some villages, there is a 90% malaria infection rate, which means not only expenditures for medicines but also days missed from school and work, further exacerbating the struggle to get ahead.

The partnership with People to People (P2P), providing funding and expertise, helped the empowered and highly motivated Rotarian businesswomen of Yumbe to implement water and sanitation programs that significantly reduced preventable illnesses in their first adopted village – Achiba. Instances of waterborne diseases were reduced from 78% of the population to 5% in the first year. The average hours spent daily to fetch water was reduced from four to one hour. In addition, all 612 residents were tested for malaria, and the 356 who tested positive were treated. As of the two-year anniversary of the Achiba intervention, the village is 98% malaria-free, and recent cases of diarrhea have been reduced to zero.

Addressing Health Challenges at the Community Level

Local health officials, who have focused only on treating people who came to health centers, are learning from the Rotarians that malaria is best fought at the community level. If everyone is tested, treated and cured within a five-mile radius, there are no longer any infected people for mosquitoes to bite and pass on the disease. In Yumbe, Uganda, Chris is working with the local Rotary Club to eradicate malaria, village by village.

Members of the Rotary Club of Yumbe are all leaders of Women's Village Savings and Loan Associations (VSLAs) who receive micro-loans from TCP Global. Once they have enough money to feed their children and pay school fees, they feel they have left extreme poverty behind and are ready to give back to their communities. They are P2P's eyes and ears and sleeves rolled up on the ground. They solicit requests from villages committed to improving their quality of life. For some villages, that means there will be latrines for the first time, so residents no longer defecate in the open. There will be handwash stations. There will be accessible water sources providing safe water and filters to make that water clean at the household level. As a direct result, there will be less disease, less absenteeism, and less money wasted in treating diseases that need not exist.

The Rotarians coordinate with and assist Village Health Teams to test and treat all villagers for malaria. They provide workshops for health, hygiene, maternal and child care, and workshops to reduce domestic violence. They have the connections locally to provide villagers with whatever resources they request. They don't look to Chris for everything. They take the initiative. They innovate. Many of the VSLAs use their interest earnings to pay for transport for pregnant women to get prenatal care and to make it to a birthing center for delivery. Once they have adequate resources, they plan to upgrade that transport from a bumpy ride on a moto-bike to a bumpy ride on a seat in a side-car of a moto-bike. They also pay a health worker to check on the baby during the first week. No one asked them to do this. They saw a problem and implemented a solution.

This is a sea-change in behavior. One of our borrowers told us she had been reluctant to even speak out in parent meetings at her children's school. Since she was often behind in paying fees, she felt she had no right to have a voice. Now, the women speak out, and people listen. They have status in the community and their homes. In the network of over 1,000 borrowers who receive TCP Global loans are some with relatives in government positions. At the very least, these connections will help women navigate government bureaucracies. At best, it will get them a seat at the table where decisions are made.

Strength in Numbers

There is strength and power in numbers. When the TCP Global borrowers walk through town in their uniform shirts, people take notice. When visitors from the capital, 12 hours away in Kampala, come to town, the district officials take them to see the women's work in the villages. Based on their success in the first village, Achiba, the chief medical officer at the nearby Bidibidi Camp for

South Sudanese refugees, modified the way health services are provided to the 240,000 residents of the camp. Yumbe Rotarians are making a difference and inspiring others to open up to new possibilities.

Case in point: Smart Centre Group is committed to "Training the local private sector in Simple, Market-based, Affordable, and Repairable Technologies." They share their expertise on well-drilling techniques appropriate to each region and have 20 years of experience throughout Africa. Until Yumbe, however, they had never trained women. They are considering changes based on the positive experience with the Yumbe women.

The savvy Yumbe ladies teach me new things all the time. My parents lived through the great depression, and their resulting frugality infiltrated my DNA. When 1,000 borrowers in Yumbe invested in quality T-shirts, color coordinated to distinguish the 30 different VSLA groups, I was silently shocked. Aside from the cost of the tee shirts, I believed their colorful African dresses were far more beautiful. Then, I witnessed the impression they made in their uniform shirts as they worked in the market or walked through the streets. The uniform shirts gave them status. They were clearly identifiable as being part of something bigger than themselves.

Ripple Effects of TCP Global Loans

While TCP Global is strictly about funding micro-loans, the ripple effects include women's empowerment, clean water, malaria eradication, education, maternal and child healthcare, and a decrease in domestic violence.

If you read the short histories in this book about Rukia, Lenny, and Nafish, you will understand that no one needs to explain to them the importance of education. For generations, education has been a priority, though often unaffordable. During my 2022 visit to Yumbe, every woman I interviewed said she used increased earnings to pay school fees or enroll her children in a better school. Their other top priority was food security.

Nutrition and education are improvements that can be implemented at the household level. For families with limited resources, access to water requires a community effort. Access to water is a critical need across Africa, where girls often miss school in order to spend four to five hours each day fetching water for the family. And all too often, those water sources are not clean and may be shared with animals, creating more health risks. In the Democratic Republic of the Congo, there is the added risk of rape along the path if girls do not travel in groups.

Training Center

A problem they continue to work on is the disaffected young men with no job opportunities, few diversions and too much time on their hands. In addition to training young men to make bricks, drill wells and build latrines, the women are working to establish a training center where young men and women can learn skills to provide them with income. The problem, unfortunately, is not unique to Yumbe. Perhaps this amazing group of women can pilot a solution to share with the rest of the world.

Two Good Foundations International (GFI) representatives traveled to Yumbe in 2022 to provide workshops for the TCP Global borrowers on making liquid and bar soap and sewing reusable diapers and sanitary pads. The sanitary pads are for distribution to adolescent girls who often drop out of school due to embarrassment when they have their periods and no means to control the flow. According to the World Bank, menstruation causes 10% of girls in sub-Saharan Africa to miss up to 20% of the school year and often drop out altogether. Affordable pads are essential for keeping girls in school.[64]

The VSLA groups used some of their interest earnings to buy the molds and ingredients for the soap they now give to elderly and indigent people in their communities. They keep some soap for themselves and sell the rest in the market, thus having both a

64 Oni Lusk-Stover, et al. World Bank Blog, "Globally, periods are causing girls to be absent from school." June 27, 2016, https://blogs.worldbank.org/education/globally-periods-are-causing-girls-be-absent-school

sustainable business and a charitable endeavor. They are working by Zoom with Jennifer Mally of GFI to experiment with soap additives to help repel mosquitoes. In early 2023, GFI negotiated the purchase of land to build a training center, in which GFI will train women to make soap, reusable sanitary pads and diapers, and skin lotions and train them in basic financial literacy and other topics of interest.

Weekly Zoom Rotary Meetings

TCP Global has a unique opportunity in Yumbe since both Chris and I, as well as others, attend the weekly meetings of the Rotary Club of Yumbe and learn of the issues and opportunities. We have the chance to ask questions and understand community concerns better. It is challenging to be relevant from across the world, but we make a real effort to know the community. Chris made his third trip to Yumbe in February of 2023. We have both spent time with the community leaders and come to respect their abilities and have experienced the living conditions in Yumbe. Visiting the loan sites, experiencing the living conditions and forming a personal connection with the people clearly makes for a better working relationship, but we simply do not have the resources to visit every site since we cover the costs of the trips from our personal funds.

We help as much as we can. Despite the French-English language barrier, we also found a way to add extra value to our relationship with Potentiel Terre in Niger. Zakari Hassane came highly recommended by the Returned Peace Corps Volunteer (RPCV) members of Friends of Niger, who had collaborated with him on several projects. Chris secured 60 Sawyer Water Filters, which Zakari shared among the VSLA loan programs he oversees as a fiscal agent.

In late 2022, I teamed up with Tom Lightbown, who served in Peace Corps Niger in the mid-1960s and remains deeply committed to the country. We worked closely with Zakari to develop a solid grant proposal, transferring grant application skills along the way. Zakari began by outlining what he wanted to do. The request was for water, sanitation, hygiene and women's empowerment. We asked him endless questions to fill in the details. I drew on my experience as Grants Administrator at the Port of Miami to draft the proposal, with Zakari reviewing along the way, and Tom turned our work into a highly professional presentation.

Unfortunately, that grant proposal was unsuccessful, possibly because the funder had ceased operations in Niger, but we will persist. Zakari notes that he learned a lot about the grant application process that he will undoubtedly put to good use.

What makes up the PLUS in TCP Global Plus is the work done by the many talented and motivated people who partner with TCP Global and P2P in the field after they are economically empowered through small business loans. I would like to introduce three of those remarkable people.

NAFISH ZULAIKA

When Nafish Zulaika received her first loan in May of 2021, she, her husband and their five children lived in a grass-thatched hut where the family experienced hunger and domestic violence. Two of her children were not in school. After two loans of $56 and $332 from TCP Global, her family now enjoys three meals a day, has harmony in the home, and is kept dry by a solid iron roof on the home. All the children are in school, and her farmer husband works with her in the business.

Before receiving her first loan, she sold produce from a mat in the open air, on the ground in the marketplace. Eighteen months later, she rents a room in the covered market where there is a night watchman. She employs two people and has expanded her inventory to include flour, beans, and fresh produce. Now that she can lock the door on her market space, she no longer has to carry everything back and forth to the market.

For the first time in her life, Nafish has hope for a better future. While her own education ended at secondary school, she is determined to make it possible for her children to complete their education. She also bought land to build a better house and secure her children's future.

While she has come a long way, many challenges remain, such as the need to spend four to five hours every day to fetch water from the nearest water source, five kilometers away. Akidi, the village of 600 where she lives, is plagued by malaria and water-borne diseases, as there is no way to purify the water they fetch from the stream.

Nafish is grateful that her children's lives are far better than her childhood. Her father died in an accident when she was 14, leaving her mother, a subsistence farmer with nine children to raise on her own. They lived in a conflict area where they experienced terrible hunger, and each family member had one set of clothes to wear, and those were not even proper clothes, she remembers. There was seldom money for school fees. There was no support from the government, and her mother showed signs of mental illness. Nafish says she sometimes considered suicide.

Now, she is a member of the Rotary Club of Yumbe and is working to help others who experience the types of hardship she experienced in her life.

Helping the Village of Her Birth

When Chris Roesel, director of Africa Programs for TCP Global, asked Yumbe Rotarians to help him identify communities needing WASH interventions, Nafish was among the first to respond. She completed a survey for Tiji, the village of her birth, which proved to be the neediest of all nine proposals submitted. Nafish committed to taking full responsibility for recruiting residents to dig the pits for latrines, drill the wells by hand, and construct hand-wash stations. She facilitated the admission of Tiji's Village Savings and Loan Association to the TCP Global program and committed to mentoring them to success.

Initially, her fellow Rotarians, who wanted to help villages of Rotary members, were upset that Nafish got approval for a village 45 kilometers away, where no Rotarian currently lives. Then, in March of 2023, the current and future Rotary club presidents visited Tiji and were quickly won over. A survey they conducted of twenty-six Tiji households indicated:

71% of children under 5 had diarrhea in the last two weeks

86% of children under 5 had malaria

67% of the total population had malaria

19% of income was spent on diarrhea treatment

67% of income was spent on malaria treatment

Income was $0.36/pp/day.

While survey questions about expenses and earnings are not considered 100% reliable, they accurately reflect that a high percentage of family income is spent treating preventable diseases. Nafish's intervention is just in time. A new law affecting their parish (county) will soon take one goat from any household that does not have a latrine. The households do not have latrines, partly because they cannot afford them, and losing a goat will make it all the more difficult. With roughly $20,000 from P2P, Nafish is administering projects to provide not only latrines but clean water filters to serve every household and a well to replace the dirty water source that contributes to the high rate of diarrhea. With their TCP Global loans and the decrease in expenditures for medicines, residents of Tiji will be able to forge a path forward.

When the survey was initially conducted, Tiji had 145 families, but two months later, due to increased fighting in Sudan just six kilometers away, an influx of refugees raised the number of families to 190. Nafish is looking for ways to stretch the project budget to accommodate the new families.

LENNY CHRISTINE

Lenny Christine exemplifies the tremendous rewards to be reaped by investing in the entrepreneurial poor. She has a big heart, native intelligence, and boundless energy for service, which she says comes from her mother and her Muslim faith. TCP Global micro-loans helped her improve her income to feed, educate, and house her family and then turn her attention to community service. As a healthcare professional, she coordinates the efforts of the Rotary Club of Yumbe with the district health officials and organizes projects to eradicate malaria in several villages. She is also a subsistence farmer. In February of 2023, she participated in training to become one of Yumbe's first six female water engineers. She elaborated on the training during the February 15th Rotary Club of Yumbe meeting.

They drilled down two meters in the first two hours and reached nine meters on day two. They planned to go to 15 meters so there would be water year-round, but the soil kept collapsing at the lower depths. The Malawi instructor showed them how to install a casing to hold the soil. The lengthy drilling process gave them lots of time to ask questions and learn from the expert. If he had any doubts about the value of training women, they quickly dissipated.

While the drilling progressed over three days, the women learned useful information about wells from hands-on experience as they repaired a nearby well that had ceased functioning. They removed rusty, worn-out pipes, cleaned out the mud that clogged the pipe and put the well back in working order. These are all useful skills, allowing the Yumbe Rotarians to be more effective in training villagers to maintain their new wells.

As with most efforts in Yumbe, the Rotarians were gracious in sharing their good fortune with others from Rotary clubs as far as Kampala, 12 hours south of Yumbe. In all, there were 15 trainees, including one from South Sudan, who planned to share what he learned with family members in the nearby Bidibidi camp for Sudanese refugees.

Acceptance of Refugees

Lenny Christine believes that residents of Yumbe District are unique in their inclusion and warm acceptance of refugees. Sudanese residents of the Bidibidi Refugee camp, 15 kilometers from the town of Yumbe, make up almost 30% of the one million population of Yumbe District. There are dozens of international organizations whose signs block the view from roads leading in and out of town. Those organizations neither benefit Yumbe nor hire people from Yumbe. They all have big Land Rovers to commute to Bidibidil. Yet, there is no apparent animosity or jealousy toward the refugees, only empathy.

Most people in Yumbe, including Lenny Christine, were refugees at some time. While some forget the difficult times and turn their backs on the less fortunate when their situation improves, the people of Yumbe do not. Mostly, they remember the kindness they were shown when they were refugees and are paying back in kind.

The fact that the Yumbe Ugandans are 80% Muslim, while the Sudanese refugees are majority Christian is not an issue. The only time they had a problem was when the refugees started cutting all the trees to make charcoal for cooking. That was upsetting, but they worked it out, and the Sudanese stopped cutting trees. They did not let the "otherness" of the refugees get in the way of resolving differences.

Despite her family's warm welcome as refugees in the Democratic Republic of the Congo (DRC), Lenny Christine remembers her entire childhood as a prolonged "terrible" time. Her parents were very poor. Her father was a peasant farmer, and her mother supplemented their income by brewing alcohol. The children's education was a priority, but Lenny Christine had long, hard days. She started by fetching water, which was a three-kilometer round trip. Then she cleaned the compound where they lived, went to school, played volleyball and then came home to help her mother make nguli, a local alcoholic beverage made from fermented maize, flour and yeast.

Her father was very protective and spirited her out of the DRC when she entered adolescence. Once she started to develop breasts, he knew he had to get her out of the DRC before someone would carry her off as a "bride," so he brought her back to the relative safety of Northern Uganda. After her mother died, she was reunited with the family and helped her father raise her four brothers and three sisters. Her father managed to educate them all. Lenny says she always worked very hard and was highly motivated and eventually earned a master's degree in public health through a distance-learning course.

She worked for the government health department at one point, but the salary was very low. Her husband also had a low salary, so Christine took a loan to make local bread. Now, she has retail and wholesale bread customers in Yumbe and several villages. However, since she has not worked for a salary, she does not qualify for a retirement program and is working hard to secure her future. In addition to bread-making, she buys land to increase the size of her farm, located 15 kilometers from her home. She has 20 goats and 18 sheep on the farm and raises cassava, a staple in Northern Uganda. She would like to find a way to help Kenna, the farming community where she owns farmland. Currently, Kenna has no easily accessible water and no latrines.

Education as a Top Priority

While her three youngest children attend affordable private schools in Yumbe District, she is doing well enough to send her older children to better private schools in larger towns. One son is studying medicine in a five-year program in Kampala. The other two study four hours away in Arua, where one is completing secondary school and the other studies law.

In 2019, when she joined the AMANGABO Savings group, she was just beginning construction of the concrete-block house with an iron roof and glass windows where she now lives. In May of 2021, when she improved her income after receiving a TCP Global loan, she immediately moved her children from free government schools to private schools, which provided better education opportunities.

Lenny Christine belongs to the AMANGABO savings group, which means "woke" and is a founding member of the Rotary Club of Yumbe, which received its charter on April 7, 2022. She played a key role in implementing the club's "adopt a village" project as their way of "giving back." She gave workshops on child and maternal health and other health-related topics, coordinated with the

District Department of Health and the Village Health teams to test everyone in Achiba Village for malaria and then treated over 50% of the residents who tested positive. In late 2022, the Yumbe Club adopted a second village, Ramadah, and a third in early 2023.

The AMANGABO group uses interest earnings on the loans they manage to do charity work in their village. They support the elderly with donations of food and clothes and hire moto-taxis to ensure pregnant women get to the health facility to receive the prenatal care they need. They take expectant mothers to a birthing center for delivery and pay the Village Health Team to monitor newborns in the home for the first week and have noted a decline in infant mortality. Lenny Christine also provides health-related workshops in her village.

Additional loan-program earnings are used to buy materials to teach villagers to weave mats and do other local crafts, which they can then sell for profit. AMANAGABO members also teach villagers to make liquid and bar soap.

While international organizations typically come in with their staff and their programs already designed, by contrast, when Women's Village Savings and Loan Associations (VSLAs) decide to embark on community service, the first thing they do is sit down with the community and ask what they want.

Lenny Christine is grateful to TCP Global for the loans that have helped her increase her income and for introducing her to Rotary.

Rotary is a very important part of her life. She says, "Rotary is important because it connects us with the rest of the people in the world. Rotary creates a more positive environment for promoting world peace, encourages people to be ethical and honest. It helps people understand humanity and cultural awareness and promotes equity between men and women, making sure that all have a voice." She says Rotary has also helped them "improve their leadership and their ability to manage themselves." It is hard to imagine a more passionate promoter of Rotary than Lenny Christine in Yumbe, Uganda. In March, she attended Rotary President-Elect

Training (PETS) to prepare for her year as President of the Rotary Club of Yumbe for 2023-24.

RUKIA DRICIRU

Rukia came a long way in three short years. In 2019, she sold second-hand clothes from a mat on the street and slept on the ground in her grass-thatch home. In November of 2022, she was featured in the Rotarian Magazine, distributed worldwide, as president of a Rotary Club that stands out in serving humanity.

This is not her first dramatic turnaround. When she was three, her parents fled with Rukia and her three brothers to the relative safety of the Democratic Republic of Congo as they waited out the worst of the Idi Amin war years in Uganda. After their return, three years later, she learned valuable life lessons as she observed her mother's struggle to nurture the family on her own while her father was absent for long periods of time in Kampala, the capital city of Uganda. Even in 2023, the trip from Yumbe to Kampala is an arduous day-long journey. Thirty-five years ago, transportation was much slower, more unpredictable, and less accessible.

Like Rukia, her mother was a businesswoman. Her mother bought fish in the countryside and sold it in the Arua Market in the Arua District of Uganda to earn enough money to get by. It was not easy on her own, but her mother managed to pay for medicines, school fees and feed and clothe a family that eventually included three boys and three girls. Rukia remembers there was lots of hunger in their home, but she also remembers what little they had; her mother shared with children from other families who were hungry. Sharing and caring for others, she says, is rooted in their Muslim tradition. "Caring for Humanity" is now emblazoned on the back of the shirts she had made for the Rotary Club of Yumbe. As in her mother's household, these are not mere words.

First President of the Yumbe Rotary Club

Rukia is a founding member and first president of the Rotary Club of Yumbe, whose charter was approved on April 7, 2022, the same day Katanje Brown Jackson was confirmed as the first African-American Supreme Court Justice in the United States. Those two ground-breaking events are forever linked in my mind.

The many good works of the Yumbe Rotary Club are detailed elsewhere in this book. Each of the women in the Rotary Club represents a Woman's Village Savings and Loan Association (VSLA), whose 30 to 60 members also do good work. The VSLAs use the interest from the loans they manage to provide food and supplies for the elderly and transportation to ensure that pregnant women receive prenatal medical care.

They train young village boys and others to make the mats that others buy to sleep on somewhat more comfortably on dirt floors in thatched-grass huts. They train young boys to make eco-friendly bricks using a Makiga Brick machine, and they plan to train them in digging more affordable wells, using improved technology developed in Malawi, with the intent of providing the young men more opportunities to earn a decent living.

Affordable, conveniently located wells are needed to reduce the time spent each day to fetch water. While some women and girls spend up to six hours a day fetching water, Rukia has fortunately arrived at a stage where she can pay someone to fetch water for her.

How Did She Get Here?

In early 2020, a friend invited her to join the ASITE savings group. At that time, she lived in a thatched house whose roof needed constant, costly repair and replacement. She slept on a mat on the dirt floor, along with the three children of her late brother, all of whom she is raising on her own. She was able to save just a little over one dollar per week from her work sitting in the street, selling second-hand clothes, near the Yumbe Market.

In November 2020, when ASITE became part of the TCP Global micro-loan program, she received her first loan, which she used to rent a kiosk and escape the dust, sun, and rain of the street location.

As of January 2023, Rukia had received four loans and now has two kiosks and one concrete block room with a lockable door. She employs two people to run the kiosks during the day and pays another to guard the kiosks at night to protect the merchandise. She now sells new and used clothing and saves nearly $30 each week, which she receives back with interest each December and uses to make major purchases in Kampala. She resells those items when the price is right in Yumbe.

As a result of her hard work and a small amount of capital from TCP Global (four loans averaging $278 in the first two years) to improve her business, Rukia now has a permanent concrete-block home with an iron-sheet roof. She and each of her three adopted children sleep on a bed with a mattress in their own room. She even has rooms that she sometimes rents out. Thanks to a water filter she received through a Rotary Club project supported by People to People (P2P), they have clean water to drink.

It has been a winding journey to get where she is today. As a young married woman, she and her husband both worked in Yumbe District government offices, but the pay was so poor that she left to work in Sudan, where the larger salary enabled her to send money to her father to help pay for her brother's university education. After working for four years for the Loka Women Association, an organization that empowered women, she returned to Uganda when war broke out in Sudan. While she has no children of her own and is now separated from her husband, she accepted responsibility for her brother's children after he died in a vehicle accident.

Rukia thrives on Rotary and lives the Rotary Four-Way Test:

Is it the truth?

Is it fair to all concerned?

Will it be beneficial to all concerned?

Will it build goodwill and better friendships?

She says, "Rotary is about friendship," and it gives her opportunities for personal growth, developing public speaking skills, and sharing and learning from other women. Rukia says she proudly wears her Rotary lapel pin. As Rotarians, she and her colleagues are committed to giving back to the less fortunate.

They started with a project to eradicate malaria and water-borne diseases in one of the poorest villages and applied lessons learned to adopt subsequent villages. In weekly Rotary Zoom meetings with participants from Kansas, New York, and Florida, as well as parts of Uganda, she has an opportunity to partner with and learn from other Rotarians.

Chris Roesel, a Rotarian from Kansas and member of a Rotary E-WASH (Water sanitation, hygiene) club, facilitates the Rotary Zoom meetings and has formed deep ties with Yumbe, starting from his first of three visits in 2020. Melissa Masoner of the Topeka, Kansas, Rotary Club attends most meetings and enlisted her club to absorb the Rotary International portion of the dues for the Yumbe Club. At nearly $60 per person, this is a serious burden for a club with some members for whom that represents more than one week's earnings. I attend from Miami, and Rotary officials from Uganda often participate as well.

Together, as partners, we brainstorm solutions to the challenges the club faces in its efforts to empower local villages and avoid creating dependency. Rukia sees Rotary and these sessions as part of her continuing education. And I see working with Rukia and the empowered ladies of Yumbe as part of my continuing education. We have a great deal to learn from each other.

Earning a Living / Feeding Neighbors...*Sept 22nd*

This water pump, bought with TCP Global earnings, irrigates crops grown by the GARAKE Savings Group of the Mariah Cooperative in the Zinder region. See results in the photo at the top.

This micro-entrepreneur from the Village Savings and Loan Association, SAA buys from local gardeners and sells condiments in the local market at affordable prices.

Thus, she earns money to care for her family while supporting regional farmers and providing a valuable service to neighboring households.

NIGER - September, 2022

A May 3, 2022 *Bloomberg News Report* explains how the 'for profit' micro loan industry has spent millions in tax payer dollars to increase misery rather than reduce poverty.

Traditional lenders encourage large loans because they are more cost effective to administer.

Size Matters: < $100 vs > $1000

With an $84 loan, Balkissa bought a 25-liter can of oil and a bag of wheat flour. In the morning, she makes donuts bought by those who go to the fields. In the evening she sells to young people in her village in **Niger**.

TCP Global partners give borrowers loans they can manage successfully. As they gain experience, the loan size increases.

CHAPTER 9

Rotary: Good Work with Potential to be Better

> "This is a changing world, we must be prepared to change with it. The story of Rotary will have to be written again and again."
> *Paul Harris, founder of Rotary International*

Rotary was the vision of Attorney Paul Harris. On February 23, 1905, he started the first Rotary Club in Chicago "So professionals with diverse backgrounds could exchange ideas and form meaningful, lifelong friendships."[65] Initially, they rotated meetings among their various members – hence the name Rotary. Within 16 years, Rotary programs sprang up on six continents, and its vision expanded to include significant humanitarian service. It is hard to imagine that just over a century ago, humanitarian service included Rotarians providing latrines in Chicago.

Rotary and Chicago have come a long way since those humble beginnings in 1905, and it has not always been smooth. Rotarians did not always live up to the standards set by the Rotary 4-Way test of the things we think, say or do:

1. Is it the truth?
2. Is it fair to all concerned?

---

65 https://www.rotary.org/en/about-rotary/history

3. Will it build goodwill and better friendships?
4. Will it be beneficial to all concerned?

Women In Rotary

When Dr. Sylvia Whitlock joined the Rotary Club of Duarte, California, in 1976 as the first official female Rotarian, the club's charter was quickly rescinded by Rotary International (RI). The charter was not reinstated until the Supreme Court, in a unanimous decision in 1987, directed RI to do so, despite a loud campaign by wives of Rotarians to keep women out of their husbands' clubs.

Things moved rather quickly, and in 1988, Sylvia became the first woman to be officially recognized as president of a Rotary club; in 1989, RI welcomed women Rotarians. It then took another 34 years for Canadian Jennifer Jones to become the first female president of Rotary International. Today, it is hard to *Imagine Rotary* (the 2023 theme) without women.

Someday, I hope it will be difficult to imagine Rotary without significant participation by people from diverse economic backgrounds, as well as the diverse cultures, races, and genders, which Rotary has already committed to embracing. As the Rotary Club of Yumbe in Uganda has demonstrated, you don't have to be rich to be an effective mover and shaker in your own community. If Rotary aspires to improve the quality of life in the most underserved communities on the planet, it would do well to seek partnerships with more leaders like the women of Yumbe. They are certainly out there.

Outside-the-Box Thinking for Best Results

Since its Global Polio Eradication Mission was launched in the Philippines in 1979, Rotary members have contributed over $2 billion and donated countless volunteer hours to vaccinate nearly 3 billion children in 122 countries and virtually eliminate polio in all countries except Pakistan and Afghanistan. This required considerable 'outside-the-box' thinking along the way, and a similar approach is needed to address Rotary's seven areas of focus successfully:

- Peace and conflict prevention/resolution.
- Disease prevention and treatment.
- Water and sanitation.
- Maternal and child health.
- Basic education and literacy.
- Economic and community development.
- Protecting the environment

To achieve these ambitious goals, it is necessary to reach communities where the problems are endemic, as Rotary did with polio. Rotary could spend *billions* sending delegations into those communities to implement projects or spend *millions* (or less) supporting grassroots efforts by empowered citizens living in those communities. It won't be easy, but taking on polio was not a simple challenge either.

According to the Multi-Dimensional Poverty Index Report 2022 for Uganda, published by Oxford University, "The Northern region [of Uganda] has the highest level of multidimensional poverty at 62.9%." The Rotarians of Yumbe, working at the grassroots level, are making headway on all seven Rotary areas of focus in this poorest of regions.

In less than three years, TCP Global invested $213,000 in Women's Village Savings and Loan Associations in the Yumbe District of Northern Uganda. The micro-loan investment is intended to help entrepreneurs in the region improve their businesses, increase their incomes, improve their families' quality of life, and provide earnings for their fiscal agent to do community improvement projects. Instead of sending in programs, the TCP Global approach is to economically empower people to remove the chains of abject poverty to improve their lives and communities.

Yumbe Rotarians Address All Seven Rotary Areas of Focus

The entrepreneurs who receive TCP Global loans universally report spending increased earnings on educating their children, eliminating hunger from their homes, and improving their businesses. They report a dramatic decline in domestic violence once financial worries subside. Thus, the TCP Global investment empowers the community to address three of Rotary's seven focus areas. After the women decided to form the Rotary Club of Yumbe, they did community clean-ups, planted trees, began adopting villages to fight malaria and waterborne diseases and provided access to clean water, checking off three more areas of focus.

With guidance and financial support from Rotary E-WASH cadre member Chris Roesel, they adopted a series of villages to improve access to water and then provided filters to ensure the cleanliness of that water. They worked with the Village Health Teams to test for malaria and treat those who tested positive. One of the Rotarians, who holds a Master's Degree in Public Health, leads workshops on maternal and child health and other health-related topics. '

VSLA borrowers repay their loans with interest, which the group then uses for community projects. Many VSLAs use TCP Global earnings to improve maternal and child health, the last of the seven Rotary focus areas. VSLA loan program earnings cover the transport cost for pregnant mothers to get prenatal checkups and to reach a birthing center for delivery. Earnings are also used to pay a Village Health Team worker to follow up on newborns. While there are no official surveys to document the impact of these interventions, women report a decline in infant mortality.

TCP Global loan recipients universally report that paying their children's school fees, usually at the more expensive private schools they find superior, is a top priority. As mentioned previously, they report a significant decline in domestic violence because "poverty breeds violence." Increasing wealth does not put an end to violence, but eliminating economic uncertainty and giving people hope contributes to increased harmony in the home. As of early 2023, the Rotarians of Yumbe are working to provide opportunities for young men in hopes of reducing drug use and the violence associated with drug activities. Whatever approach they come up with is likely to be as, or more effective, than programs designed in Western capitals and much less costly.

Connecting Yumbe Rotarians to the World

The Yumbe Rotarians take the lead but are eager to connect with and learn from the rest of the world. Their weekly Rotary Zoom meetings are attended by Uganda Rotarians from more established clubs in larger cities and by international Rotarians as well. Rukia Driciru, a founder and first president of the Rotary Club of Yumbe, is grateful for the opportunity to learn from and share experiences with other women. We can all learn from our own mistakes, but it is far more advantageous to learn from the mistakes of others. Outside Rotarians on the weekly calls have come to respect the abilities of the Yumbe Rotarians and are careful about offering "advice," but they have become skilled at asking the right questions.

Respectful questions helped the members recognize the importance of empowering, rather than creating dependency in the villages they adopted, and pressuring the government for goods and services that were approved but not forthcoming, rather than accepting defeat and looking for alternatives.

Economic Empowerment as the Basis for Development

It all starts with economic empowerment. As long as a woman's family suffers from hunger and her children cannot attend school, fixing those immediate problems consumes her time and energy. Once those challenges are addressed, there is a wealth of talent, ability, and energy to attack other problems.

When The Colombia Project contemplated going global, I feared that the rest of the world's impoverished people might not be as great an investment as Colombians, known for their entrepreneurial skills. Mayans in remote villages of Guatemala quickly proved me wrong. Again, I have that same nagging feeling that maybe the Yumbe women are unique and that we will not see that same "service above self" generosity of spirit in other communities. Surely, it will not be the same everywhere and may not exist in some regions, but it is worth our while to find out.

That $213,000 initial investment by TCP Global empowered more than 1,000 entrepreneurs to improve their incomes and working conditions, improve the housing and sleeping arrangements for the family, eliminate hunger and keep all their children in school. Another $20,000 from P2P and $30,000 from two grants have yielded significant results in all seven Rotary areas of focus in four targeted villages with a total population of 3,500:

Cut the malaria infection rate in half in four villages

Increased access to latrines from 35% to 99% in four villages

Increased access to a hand-wash station from 10% to 99%

Decreased reported incidences of diarrhea in those under 5 from 50%t to 5%

Implemented maternal and infant-care programs in 25 Rotarian villages

For their April 19, 2023 meeting,[66] Yumbe Rotarians were joined by Rotarians zooming in from Kampala and Arua in Uganda, Kansas, New York, Maryland, and Florida, to hear updates on villages adopted for a full range of WASH programs, plus five villages for malaria eradication. I doubt there is a Rotary Club on the planet that could match them for tireless efforts or effective results. In the previous week, they convened a meeting of 14 district officers, nine sub-county officers, eight Rotarians, and two representatives of CCEDUC, a grassroots non-profit, to coordinate efforts in the Yumbe District. This meeting included 18 women and 15 men.

In Oyaru, they held a meeting attended by 123 villagers to discuss top priorities (latrines and access to water) and a plan forward.

66 https://www.youtube.com/watch?v=bEWcXVZ4TfM.

Villagers said it was the first time anyone had offered to help them improve their community.

In the previous week, they had also worked on an agreement with Caritas to drill a Mzuzu well and use the opportunity to train additional well-drillers. They reported that due to intense fighting in Sudan, Tiji, one of their adopted villages, had grown by 25 new families from Sudan, just a few kilometers north, in the previous week. The husband of their representative to parliament, for whom the Rotarians had installed a well, agreed to transport supplies from Kampala to Tiji for the new Tiji wells. Rotarians shared their plan for mobilizing four additional villages next week.

A representative from Ramadah Village presented a list of materials needed to construct 47 latrines and hand-wash stations, and two hand-drilled Mzuzu wells at $800 each (versus $7,000 for machine-dug, deep bore-hole wells).

In Machangana, young men trained in brick making prepared to build latrines during the following week, after the Eid al-Fitr celebrations, to mark the end of Ramadan. Because they are part of the community, the Yumbe Rotarians find ways to address multiple community concerns with each project. Providing better access to water means young girls have time to attend school. Finding meaningful work for young men means fewer disaffected youth straying into anti-social activities. This is not a job for the Yumbe Rotarians. They are part of the community and deeply invested in its welfare. All of this was on the agenda for just one meeting of the Rotary Club of Yumbe.

If we unleash the potential that exists in marginalized communities, we may find many more future Rotarians with the wisdom, energy and commitment necessary to solve their problems with minimal outside resources. Instead of providing health, water, sanitation, environmental, and education programs, what if Rotary economically empowered natural leaders in those communities so that they could be partners rather than program beneficiaries?

How Rotary Could Replicate the Yumbe Experience

1. Encourage more affluent Rotary Clubs to adopt impoverished communities, provide affordable loans to empower the people to lift themselves out of poverty and then follow the lead of the local people, supporting their efforts to reach their goals. If any of them elect to become Rotary clubs, help them pay their dues. The Rotary Club of Topeka, Kansas, pays the RI dues for the Yumbe Rotary Club. The $60 annual fee may seem modest on a developed world salary, but to a market vendor who feels rich if income reaches $100 per week, it is onerous. Rotary could consider scholarships and encourage clubs from wealthy districts to fund those scholarships for Rotarians from impoverished communities.
2. Change the Rotary policy that requires micro-loan funds to be channeled through a registered MFI. In marginalized communities far from population centers, those MFI loans are usually not affordable and often harm rather than help the borrowers. As one of our borrowers explained, 'I felt I was working for [the MFI] instead of my family.' In Yumbe, the Rotarian VSLAs charge less than 1% per month, while there is considerable evidence that MFIs charge over 10% per month.

The Yumbe women are not the only ones who recognize the problem with some MFIs. The May 3, 2022, report in Bloomberg News notes that "Government aid agencies, commercial banks, nonprofits and socially minded investment firms are pouring record amounts—more than $50 billion of committed funds in 2020, industry data show—into an international array of lenders. The infusion of capital has continued despite annualized interest rates that can top 100% and aggressive debt-collection tactics that have left some borrowers homeless. The Himalayan News Service of February 14, 2023, echoes the Bloomberg findings, reporting that of 78 suicide victims in the Sudurpaschim Province, 44 were driven to suicide by high interest and predatory practices by micro-loan agencies, practices to which the banking authorities are reportedly "turning a blind eye."

Under existing Rotary policy, the VSLA groups, including those headed by Rotarians, do not qualify to manage Rotary micro-loan funds, despite their 100% good repayment record with TCP Global loan funds and the low interest they charge. Since TCP Global, through its fiscal agent partners, builds sustainable loan programs through VSLA groups that manage the loan programs, we cannot apply for Rotary International grant support. We could only qualify if we involved one of the offending entities described in the Himalayan News and the Bloomberg report.

3. Focus on:

- Projects that fix problems sustainably rather than raise awareness. It does not help to be more aware of a problem without the resources to fix the problem;
- Understanding rather than teaching. It may be that we have more to learn than to teach;
- Empowering locals to identify the problems and develop the solutions;
- Individual circumstances rather than the one-size-fits-all approach;
- Appropriate technology.

Rotary Membership

This could be a win-win for Rotary and impoverished communities. Rotary wants to increase membership. If we move beyond affluent areas to find new Rotarians among leaders in areas struggling to get ahead, Rotary projects will be more affordable, more impactful, and more sustainable. Rotary could shift a small amount of funds from projects to supporting Rotarians in marginalized communities.

There are wise and energetic leaders in marginalized communities already living by the four-way test and ready for "service above self" to improve their communities. They understand from experience that they will likely be on the menu if they do not have a place at the table. To fully implement the seven areas of focus in the most underserved communities, Rotary would do well to give local leaders a place at the table where problems, priorities, and solutions are identified. People capable of surviving on under two to five dollars per day can also help Rotary stretch its dollars to the max.

TCP Global borrowers are one potential source of prospective Rotarians. Many more pathways are waiting to be discovered within the vast Rotary network. Clubs already partnering with exceptional grassroots organizations on Global Grants could be incentivized to sponsor new clubs, with those grassroots organizations as the nucleus. Rotary clubs in large cities in Africa, Asia, and Latin America, many of whose members, no doubt, come from poor regions, could bring Rotary to those regions to offer not charity but partnership. Personal connections make a great starting point. Rotarians are masterful at making connections. Rotary International support is essential for this type of expansion to occur on any scale.

Peace Corps Volunteers as Future Rotarians

Rotary-Peace Corps collaborations are discussed in more detail in the next chapter, but implications for Rotary membership are relevant here. Rotary membership has been virtually static for the last twenty years, with declines in the U.S. and other developed countries offset by growth in developing countries. If Peace Corps Volunteers (PCVs) were involved in effective projects supported by Rotarians, they would be more likely to join the Rotary back home. While a Peace Corps salary (I earned $7 a day in Slovakia) makes the payment of Rotary dues problematic for volunteers in the field, Rotary could offer a scholarship for PCVs as an investment in future growth. Many returning PCVs have already found their way to Rotary. Many others who currently do not know that Rotary exists might well do the same.

Since PCVs predominantly serve in rural areas, their affiliation with Rotary would help Rotary connect to rural sites where the need is greatest.

Rotary Community Corps (RCC)

The Rotary Club of Yumbe established a Rotary Community Corps (RCC) in Achiba, the first village it adopted, to ensure that the well and filters are maintained and that they continue the fight against malaria. As funds become available, they will provide the RCC with T-shirts with the Rotary logo so they feel empowered as project leaders and are easily recognized in the community. The RCCs offer the advantage of establishing a connection to Rotary without incurring fees.

And how will this be "beneficial to all concerned," the fourth item on the Rotary four-way test? It will benefit the villagers, but it will also stretch Rotary dollars and could energize donor clubs from affluent communities by partnering them with enthused Rotarians. I am always energized by my Wednesday morning Zoom meetings with the Rotary Club of Yumbe and, occasionally, fight back happy tears. They constantly amaze me with their service initiatives, boundless energy, efficiency, and willingness to share. Whenever they have something good, they look for ways to share it with others.

With local Rotarians volunteering their service and oversight, for $20,000, Rotary will provide an adopted Ugandan village of roughly 600 people, for example, with:

1. Accessible water source, relieving women and girls from fetching water, which can take up to five hours per day (allowing girls to attend school);
2. Filtered water for 10 years;
3. Sufficient latrines to eliminate defecation in the open;
4. Hand-wash stations convenient to everyone;
5. Universal testing for malaria and treatment of all who are infected;
6. For 30 TCP Global borrowers and their families, increased income to ensure that hunger is eliminated from their homes and sufficient income is available to keep all children in school;

7. Transport to prenatal care and a birthing center for all pregnant women, with follow-up monitoring of newborn babies, paid with VSLA group interest earnings.

Obstacles to Rotary Participation

Rotarians contribute in different ways. Some give money. Some give hands-on service. Some give both. While both are important, we let slide those people who only give money with a smattering of guilt-tripping. Yet those, like the Yumbe women, who give abundant service are made to understand that failure to pay dues is a deal-killer.

Rotary needs to decide if this is the best way forward or if a scholarship program for exceptional situations is in order. Sensitivity to the level of financial participation possible for economically challenged Rotarians will help.

District representatives at Yumbe Rotary Club meetings frequently pressure Yumbe Rotarians to participate in a marathon, buy Rotary shirts and contribute to various Rotary initiatives with no regard for the significant financial burden placed on Yumbe members. Chris and I try to reassure them that what they are doing is already above and beyond what many Rotary clubs accomplish and not to feel bad about not participating in every aspect of Rotary.

Were it not for the Rotary dues, membership in the Yumbe club would increase. The $60 to RI is huge for them and, fortunately, is currently paid by the Rotary Club of Topeka, Kansas. However, even the dues in Uganda are problematic for entrepreneurs one step removed from extreme poverty. What does not seem to be a problem for them is rolling up their sleeves and working in the trenches to help improve the lot of their fellow man.

The Rotary Club of Yumbe currently includes only Ugandans, but they work closely to support nine Village Savings and Loan Associations (VSLAs) in the nearby Bidibidi camp for South Sudanese refugees. They would likely be interested in sponsoring a Rotary Club in the camp for the refugees who have already been there three years, with no end in sight, were it not for the financial burden presented by the Rotary dues structure. Many formerly successful people in the camp could contribute to building a better life in the camp with a bit of outside support.

There is no question that the Rotarians in Yumbe are empowered and inspired by the connection to Rotarians in their country and worldwide. Their great work would not be possible without the financial support provided by P2P and TCP Global or mentoring by Rotarians. In working with the Yumbe Club, E-WASH Rotarian Chris Roesel drew on the information in his book, "How to Improve the World Quickly." Few things are more rewarding to a development worker, Rotarian, or writer than seeing positive results as the fruits of their labor. For that, he can thank the Yumbe Rotarians.

Sudanese Refugees Receive TCP Global Loans in Uganda... August 17, 2023

Meeting of newly-arrived Sudanese refugees who have increased Tiji Village by 25%. Yumbe Rotary Club members are working to make Tiji a healthy community. TCP Global micro-loans recently came to Tiji as well.

This was the only source of drinking water in Tiji.

Rotarians are drilling a well for clean water. Water filters and latrines are underway. Above, Rotarians prepare to deliver mosquito nets.

South Sudanese refugees who have been in the Bidibidi Refugee Camp for up to 6 Years are building new lives.

Refugee borrowers make their monthly repayments so other members can receive loans as well.

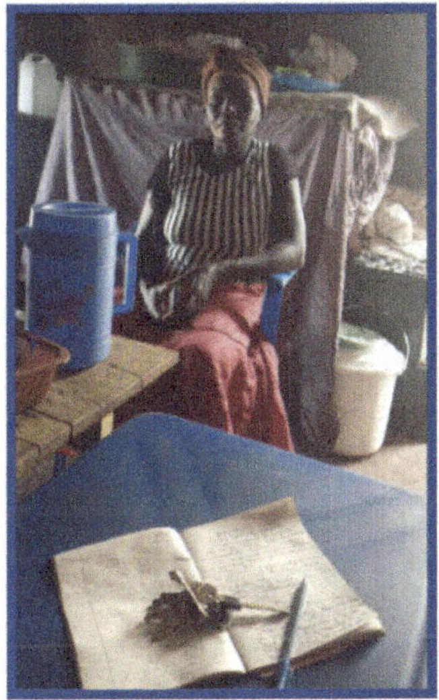

Janet is a member of "Voice of Change" savings group in Bidibidi. She used her 1st TCP Global loan to open a small hotel. Six months later, she used earnings to buy goats.

Janet now has four goats and plans to increase that to 20-30 as her second income-generating activity She says "Long live TCP Global"

Betty, a South Sudanse Refugee in Bidibidi Refugee camp says TCP Global loans changed her life.

Betty progressed from selling at the side of the road in 2021 to selling from her own store. She and her children moved from sleeping on mats to mattresses. They now have plenty to eat.

After buying two large solar cells, she earns $7-$8 per day just from charging cell phones.

Dramuke, of the "Be Alone" savings group in the Bidibidi Camp for Sudanese Refugees, received 4 loans of $100 to $500.

The loans enabled her to expand and improve her fruit and vegetable stand. With increased earnings, she was able to build a home and enroll her son in boarding school.

Members of the PHIKU savings group used interest earnings to buy 4 acres to grow cassava.

Food rations in the camp have been cut and may be discontinued.

They are preparing for the future.

CHAPTER 10

Peace Corps: Increased Emphasis on Local Empowerment

"[Senator Christopher] Dodd is calling for the Peace Corps to go backward and forward. It must go backward to the qualities of the bold, fearless men who created the unique institution. And it must go forward to become a lean, tough, expanded organization ready to leave the foxholes of caution and march forward into the glorious unknown and unknowable."
From a June 25, 2009 essay by Laurence Leamer (Nepal 1965-67) published by the Huffington Post.

In Slovakia, in the late 90s, fellow Peace Corps Volunteers (PCVs) in the Small Business Development program lamented the lack of opportunities to actually *do* small-business development. Instead, we were placed with non-profit organizations or in government offices. The Peace Corps changed the program name from Small Business Development to Community and Economic Development (CED), but the disconnect continues. It is difficult to conceive of economic development without an infusion of cash. How does one start a business, rent a space, and buy equipment and inventory without a loan unless you are already wealthy? Peace Corps service is about helping people who often live hand to mouth to get to the point where they can invest in building a better future, but by avoiding micro-loans, the Peace Corps is missing a critical tool in its anti-poverty tool kit.

TCP Global: a Good Match for CED Volunteers

TCP Global would seem to be a perfect match for CED volunteers, but it could work for any volunteer working with an effective grassroots organization. We work in small communities like those where Peace Corps Volunteers are assigned, partnering with grassroots organizations, much like those in which Peace Corps Volunteers work.

One major difference is that we offer a tangible investment in their economic development. We establish permanent loan pools to provide affordable loans to marginalized entrepreneurs in perpetuity. Earnings from running the loan programs fund community improvement projects and can also be used as matching funds for larger grants. This seems tailor-made for Community and Economic Development (CED) programs. A former Peace Corps language instructor agrees and is arranging partnerships between TCP Global and small community-based organizations in remote regions throughout Nepal.

The 21st-century Peace Corps is a far cry from your grandfather's Peace Corps; in this case, that is a real shame. Sargent Shriver, the genius behind the Peace Corps, would hardly recognize the risk-averse agency his progeny has become. Sarge had a bold vision and was fearless in placing his trust in young Americans to adapt, innovate, and thrive in diverse settings worldwide. With the best of country directors, there is still the flexibility for PCVs to try new and bold ideas. With others, there is a rigid adherence to guidelines established, it would appear, with little consideration of the needs of communities that could use help. To my horror, I was once informed by a Peace Corps program manager, "Your program gets good results, but it does not align with the metrics we have established for our CED program."

What did align with her metrics was "the number of people trained." The fact that her volunteers gave training and conducted workshops, and equipped people with information they might have little hope of applying was apparently irrelevant. To make matters worse, according to David Mayo, who served in various capacities with the Peace Corps in six countries over the last 25 years, the Peace Corps now gives more weight to the voices of "experts" instead of the local community and its volunteers. Mayo writes that "Trust in the initiative and resilience of volunteers has wavered," along with "the substitution of activities scripted by outside experts for those designed by host communities aided by volunteers.[67]

This suggests a paternalistic, "we know better than you, what you need" attitude. One goal of this book is to encourage a new attitude of respect for the abilities of people trapped in poverty. People who know how to survive and raise a family on less than $2 per day know quite a bit about sound money management, for example, and perhaps are not as much in need of training as we imagine, especially if we have not consulted them as to what types of training would be helpful.

Making Minimal Demands on Borrowers' Time

In addition, impoverished people may have a lot of demands on their time. This truth came home to me clearly when visiting the home of a loan recipient in Sabanagrande, Colombia. She sold home-cooked meals from her kitchen while caring for her severely handicapped 20-something daughter, who could not speak, walk, or control any bodily functions. Despite obvious poverty in the home, the daughter was clean, well-groomed, with a big smile. The mother said she was unable to leave her daughter unattended for any prolonged period of time. She needed a loan to improve her business and increase her earnings but could not attend the training sessions some programs require before issuing a loan.

67 David F. Mayo, "Time for Peace Corps to Refocus Mission, *The Spokesman Review*, March 24, 2023. https://www.spokesman.com/stories/2023/mar/24/david-f-mayo-time-for-peace-corps-to-refocus-missi/

For struggling entrepreneurs, even if they do not have a dependent child, attending training programs may provide a hardship if they spend considerable time fetching water or tending to the needs of multiple family members in addition to growing a business. I believe there is a tendency to assume that if people are not working, they have lots of time on their hands.

I believe the opposite is true. The artist Willem de Kooning noted that, "The problem with being poor is that it takes up all your time." Before making any demands on their time, we should ensure the training serves a real purpose in their life. Training is helpful when targeted to the community's needs and conducted by people who can speak with authority on a topic, but success cannot be measured solely by how many attended the training. We need to pay more attention to what happens after they walk out of the training center.

It is not a good idea for Peace Corps Volunteers (PCVs) to be involved in screening or approving microloans, giving out loans or accepting payments, but just as Returned Peace Corps Volunteers (RPCVs) assist quite successfully via email to help grassroots organizations manage those tasks, PCVs could assist their assigned agencies behind the scenes. PCVs could help them with publicity, record keeping and then work with them on community projects supported by the non-profit's interest earnings.

Alternative to Usurious Rates

The need is obvious. In marginalized communities around the world, people take out loans at usurious rates. In Slovakia, it was the gypsy king in the fine house, lending to those in nearby hovels. In Colombia, it is the "paga diarios" or "daily lenders." The U.S. equivalent is the payday lender charging an average of 391% per annum.[68] In Medellin, Colombia, the paga diarios

68 Tom Jackson, "In Charge Debt Solution," updated March 25, 2023, .https://www.incharge.org/debt-relief/how-payday-loans-work/.

charge up to 700%[69] annually. This is consistent with what I have heard anecdotally of one-day loans being repaid with 10% or more interest. Since these lenders operate outside the law, it is difficult to get reliable statistics, and the impoverished people upon whom these lenders prey rarely have their voices heard.

Muhammad Yunus started the Grameen Bank to provide an affordable alternative to high-interest loans that left micro-entrepreneurs with barely enough earnings to pay back the loan and never enough to build a future. The entrepreneurial poor, like all entrepreneurs, need affordable loans. If there are daily lenders in the area, there is a demonstrated need for affordable micro-loans. If daily lenders are thriving in the area, there are a lot of people taking out and repaying usurious loans who would likely thrive with a low-interest alternative. And if loan-shark thugs can manage their programs successfully, any organization hosting a Peace Corps Volunteer can do the same, with far less interest charged. It is not rocket science.

Cutting the predatory lender interest rate by 75% or more through a client-focused loan program rather than a profit-motivated loan program allows entrepreneurs to begin their climb up the economic ladder of success, the very essence of the economic development that Dr. Moyo and Yumbe MP Avako Melsa recommend.

Nonprofits working effectively in marginalized communities typically have a wealth of ideas to improve their communities - *if only there were funds*. By running a small microloan program with 30 to 40 borrowers, they *will* have funds, not just once but for as long as they run the program.

This is a no-brainer for Peace Corps—funds for community projects, a morale boost for PCVs questioning the value of their service, affordable loans for micro-entrepreneurs, plus an escape from predatory lending practices that too often have dire consequences in impoverished communities. There is more at stake here than the difference between living hand to mouth and starting

69 Jack Aldane, "Micro Lender Provides Safe Loans to Colombia's Urban Poor." Development Finance, September 15, 2017, https://www.devfinance.net/micro-lender-provides-safe-loans-columbias-urban-poor/.

the climb out of poverty. Debtors unable to repay their loans have resorted to abandoning their homes or even taking their lives.

PCVs are missing a golden opportunity to help people significantly improve their lives and communities. As the TCP Global borrowers in Yumbe demonstrate, only after the entrepreneurial poor are freed from abject poverty are they energized to improve their lives and communities. Peace Corps Volunteers want to believe that their service makes a difference. It's hard to imagine a more impactful Peace Corps service than bringing economic opportunity to the unbanked, watching them prosper, seeing the improvements they make in the health, living conditions and education of their families, and then working beside them to address community concerns.

Working With Individual PCVs

So, what can we do to bring more opportunities to the entrepreneurial rural poor? Taking an incremental, conservative approach, individual PCVs could be encouraged to find existing grassroots organizations effectively serving their community. They could also seek out Women's Village Savings and Loan Associations (VSLAs) in their areas and determine if they would like larger, more frequent loans. If the grassroots organization or the VSLA has a bank account and is registered as a non-profit, they could work directly with TCP Global, and if not, they could work through a local fiscal agent. The Peace Corps Volunteers could help identify good partners and good fiscal agents. They would offer support but have no official role in the loan program.

The TCP Global reporting system is simple and highly automated, thanks to a Peace Corps Volunteer, Curt Commander, who was evacuated from Colombia in 2020 and immediately offered his services to help TCP Global automate. The automated programs Curt designed are simple but, like any new program, can seem daunting at first. PCVs could help grassroots partners with the initial adjustment. They could also work with the grassroots organization to implement projects with the earnings from the loan program.

While the loan program is a great fit for Community and Economic Development volunteers, it works for teachers, environmentalists, health volunteers, and other volunteers. Nonprofits working in all those areas typically find they can better achieve their primary mission when their clients have more household income. In small communities, nonprofits have few opportunities to set up a reliable project revenue stream. It is a win-win-win-win-win endeavor for the entrepreneurs, the non-profit, the Peace Corps, the PCV, and the community.

Peace Corps service is an emotional roller-coaster, and volunteers often struggle with self-doubt and question whether their presence makes any difference in the lives of the people in their community. Seeing entrepreneurs prosper, watching the community thrive with the increase in locally available goods and services and helping the nonprofit implement health, education, environmental and other projects gives the PCV a sense of purpose. If Yumbe is any indication of how entrepreneurs will respond in other communities, the PCV may soon have a group of empowered citizens full of ideas and ready to work with the PCV to change their world.

Opportunity for Big Changes

With the TCP Global automated systems and an existing Cooperative Agreement between Peace Corps (PC) and Rotary International (RI), there is also an opportunity to go very big. Since signing a Cooperative Agreement in 2014, PC and RI have searched for meaningful ways to collaborate. They share nearly identical focus areas, and both seek to help marginalized peoples across the globe. The Peace Corps has boots on the ground in remote settings, and while Rotary has more than 1.4 million members in 46,000 clubs in over 200 countries, they tend to concentrate in wealthier sections of cities.

Peace Corps Volunteers can provide a link for Rotarians to poor communities in their own country. This already happens on an ad-hoc basis. For example, the Rotary Club of Tbilisi, Georgia, engaged Peace Corps Volunteers (PCVs) to distribute sewing machines and optimize their utilization in 14 villages; PCVs volunteered to staff Rotary-funded health fairs in rural sites; and when a PCV needed program literature translated to a local language, Rotarians not only handled the translation but the printing and distribution as well.

Rotary projects require the direct involvement of Rotarians. The 2014 agreement encourages Rotary Clubs to support Peace Corps Partnership projects, which suggests that PCVs might someday be substituted for the required Rotarian involvement. Expansion and clarification of the 2014 agreement are in order. As of 2023, the Cooperative Agreement has been widely applauded but largely ignored when it comes to widespread project implementation.

Peace Corps Partnership Program

The existing Peace Corps Partnership program provides a way for family and friends to support community projects initiated with the support of PCVs. It is a popular program that has funded countless latrines, school libraries, science labs, and recycling programs, but it will take an act of Congress for the existing Peace Corps Partnership Program to support micro-loan programs. Peace Corps legislation includes a specific prohibition against using partnership program funds for micro-loans. Perhaps they feared PCVs would manage loan programs, which I agree would not be a good idea. However, in conversations with then Peace Corps Director Carrie Hessler-Radelet, it appears the Collaborative Agreement with Rotary provides a possible solution.

A separate Peace Corps-Rotary Partnership Program could direct Rotary donations to micro-loan sites worldwide and would not be subject to restrictive legislation. Linking Rotarians and PCVs could be a win-win-win for Rotary, PCVs and the poor. In-country Rotarians would have a link to poor communities through the PCV. The PCV would have access to Rotarian lawyers, bankers, government workers and other experts for guidance on various community challenges. The entrepreneurial poor would have access to the resources they need to develop their businesses and improve their lives. At the grassroots level, it is not just the borrower who benefits from a loan. With new small businesses, marginalized communities are slowly transformed from commercial deserts to viable communities with shops and services available.

Thanks to the automation that TCP Global implemented over the last three years, a Rotary-Peace Corps Partnership Program would have a system to provide detailed information on each loan site and a Global Summary Report, allowing for comparison across borders, languages, and currencies. Once the PCV helps the partner learn to update a simple log of loan-related transactions, the partner can submit a report of all new loans and payments by email and receive back a confirmation, with a copy to the PCV, interested Rotarians and anyone else they wish to include in the loop, with no human intervention required along the way.

The TCP Global Summary report has flags to indicate when a program is faltering and when it qualifies for more funds. Since that report converts loan activity around the world back to dollars, the PCV can make an apples-to-apples comparison. TCP Global encourages partners to reach out to each other, to share best practices and seek guidance when they have a problem. A volunteer team of TCP Global RPCV board members is also available for a free consultation to help the Peace Corps manage this new type of Partnership Program and to explain the possibilities to Peace Corps trainees.

Various Peace Corps Directors have stressed the need for data to be shared with Congress during the budgetary process to prove the effectiveness of the Peace Corps program. The micro-loan program provides lots of data backed by heartwarming stories and photos.

That is just one scenario, but there are many ways in which TCP Global and Peace Corps Volunteers could work together. We are already doing so in a few communities, but it will be an immense missed opportunity if we continue to fail to do this on a larger scale.

Helping Women Educate their Children in Sierra Leone.. May 18, 2023

"The trouble with being poor is that it takes up all your time." ... *Willem de Kooning*

Once borrowers can meet the basic needs of their families, they have the time and energy to contribute to their communities, like celebrating Africa Child's Day, hosted by WAAM.

Women in Action Against Malnutrition (WAAM) increases availability of nutritious food in the Bo District of Sierra Leone.

Centre for Advocacy and Sustainable Empowerment (CASE) advocates for women's rights in Bo, Sierra Leone.

SUMAILA is a fish monger.

Mariama, a widow, has a small shop.

CASE's TCP Global loans help women increase their income so they can keep adolescent girls in school.

TENNEH runs a small boutique.

SIA CHIOMA sells custom wigs.

CHAPTER 11

NATIONAL PEACE CORP ASSOCIATION (NPCA) - A POTENTIALLY MIGHTY VOICE

"My wife Patti and I owe so much to our service in the Peace Corps. It inspired a lifetime of public service that began in Ethiopia during the late 1960s and continued into state government in California, the Clinton Administration, and now the U.S. Congress. ... Now more than ever, Congress must support the Peace Corps' mission and realize President Kennedy's vision of generations of young Americans ready to serve their nation and make the world a better place."
Congressman John Garamendi (D-CA), co-chair of the Congressional Peace Corps Caucus

For more than 62 years, the Peace Corps has produced multiple generations of volunteers inspired and committed to a lifetime of service, eager to make the world a better place. Idealistic and entrepreneurial, with a life-transforming experience guiding their ambitions and endeavors, they are doing a lot but could do much more. I see three major areas of missed opportunities.

1. Foreign Policy: Harnessing the lived experiences and powerful voices of RPCVs to bring about meaningful change in foreign policy and foster responsible U.S. global leadership

2. Social Impact: Leveraging the entrepreneurial spirit, innovation, and mission-driven nature of RPCVs to augment our impact through social enterprises.
3. Peacebuilding: Bringing the world home and creating a better understanding of the world on the part of Americans. We've not moved the Third Goal (bringing the world back home) needle much.

For those who have not had the privilege to serve in the Peace Corps, let me start with a few insights gained through my own experience. At any gathering of those who served in the Peace Corps – we call ourselves Returned Peace Corps Volunteers (RPCVs) – you will invariably hear people say they gained far more from their experience than they gave. They likely gush affectionately for their host country, even though they may have been constant and vocal faultfinders during their two-year service.

Difficult Adjustment Period for Volunteers

That's what we humans do when we are frustrated, floundering, and unsure of ourselves. It is not easy leaving family, friends, and familiarity behind. It is not easy to leave a world where we are confident and relevant to enter a world where we are the equivalent of a toddler trying to figure things out and with no means of effective communication. The part of our brain where our ideas, insights, and innovations are stored sees countless opportunities that our foreign-language skills cannot communicate. With our thimble-full of cultural awareness, we try to ram the square pegs of our U.S. experiences into the round holes of our new reality.

Fortunately, we usually land in communities that anticipated our arrival with the eager enthusiasm of new parents keen on satisfying our every whim. They accept us and love us despite our missteps. They find our missteps entertaining, contributing to our frustration. However, with time, we gain understanding and competence, and mutual respect grows.

It is often hard to see the new forest for the foreign trees. While we are there, we still see all that could be and continue to be frustrated by the inordinate amount of time and energy required to get clean water, stay healthy, set up a meeting, and prepare a meal, not to mention develop good working relationships with people and organizations, so we can implement projects to bring about positive and sustainable improvements. Only when the struggle is over, and we return home do we appreciate the big picture.

Nostalgia

Then the nostalgia part of our brain fills with memories from a distant continent and a life we left behind, where the sweet, ripe smell of tropical fruit greeted us when our rickety bus was still two blocks from the marketplace, where the night sky served up constellations never seen at home, and shooting stars were easy to spot in the absence of city lights. Walking down any street in Colombia, I was exhilarated by a kaleidoscope of exotic sights, smells, and sounds, reminding me I was not in Kansas anymore – well, Missouri, but you get the picture.

On the way home from my office in Slovakia during my second stint with the Peace Corps, I frequently heard classical music practiced behind walls erected long before Bach, Beethoven, and Mozart were born. And one glorious evening, the medieval church bell serenade in the town center featured *El Condor Pasa*, 7,000 miles from the nearest Inca. Peace Corps is a roller-coaster ride of highs and lows, packed with unique experiences, devoid of ho-hum moments with an intensity difficult to replicate in suburban America. Volunteers tend to feel strongly about the experience.

Heady Experience for Young Volunteers

Peace Corps is possibly the first time in a volunteer's life when they are not constrained by predefined tasks. It is a heady experience being a Peace Corps Volunteer, often perceived as the resident expert on the entire outside world. Attentive audiences are eager to hear and understand what we have to say. The degree of influence experienced by a 24-year-old entry-level employee in the U.S. is dwarfed by the potential influence of a Peace Corps Volunteer, a perk not fully appreciated until the volunteer returns home to a nine-to-five job, restricted by a detailed job description. Peace Corps presents the volunteers with the unique opportunity to test how far their creativity, intelligence, people skills, and work ethic can take them, with the Peace Corps providing an arena and a safety net.

When we get home and step back, we finally understand the value of all we left behind. Regrettably, not everyone has a great experience, but if they are attending RPCV events 10 to 50 years later, chances are they were among the lucky ones who feel they grew through their service, formed a deep attachment to their host country, and are ready to go the extra mile again to support any effort to help that country prosper if given an opportunity.

JFK's Vision for the Peace Corps

When President John F. Kennedy established the Peace Corps on March 1, 1961, he envisioned a future where our nation would benefit from the experiences of hundreds of thousands of citizens returning from Peace Corps service worldwide. Their knowledge and respectful concern for other countries, perspective gained from seeing the United States through the eyes of foreigners, and their nuanced understanding of our country's place in the world would enable the United States to have a more equitable, just, informed, and therefore more successful foreign policy.

The world would be better, safer, and more prosperous if more international relations were based on mutual respect and trust rather than fear and if we prioritized building bridges rather than walls. We tend to fear what we do not understand, and we do not understand what we have not experienced on some level.

Americans' foreign travel is largely limited to two-week stops at tourist destinations or study-abroad programs in predominantly Western countries. A Second City comedy skit once portrayed Americans traveling abroad as hunkering in luxury hotels, refusing to open the curtains for fear of seeing something different. It was a gross exaggeration but carried a grain of truth. We ignore the developing world at our peril.

RPCVs could fill that information gap if we unite, find our voice, and identify common ground, where the interests of both foreign lands and the U.S. coalesce and where Republicans and Democrats can agree. Diplomacy is not a zero-sum game. The best path forward is one of mutual respect and understanding, on which we all thrive.

Over the past 62 years, more than 241,000 Americans have served in the Peace Corps in 143 foreign countries – not quite the critical mass that Kennedy envisioned, but enough to impact U.S. foreign relations, given the right conditions. National Peace Corps Association (NPCA), an alumni organization of those who served with the Peace Corps in any capacity, has represented RPCV views to Congress on issues specifically related to the Peace Corps, but RPCVs have yet to achieve the broader level of influence that Kennedy envisioned – an immense missed opportunity.

Independent Nature of PCVs

Peace Corps attracts independent self-starters who tend to move to the beat of their own drums. RPCVs excel as diplomats, elected officials, philanthropists, educators, entrepreneurs, humanitarians, and good citizens. Some seek the company of people who share their values and world view. Many become Rotarians to continue doing the type of service to humanity they did in the Peace Corps. They join fellow RPCVs in their geographic area to enjoy the fellowship of like-minded individuals who share similar intense Peace Corps experiences. Whether a volunteer served in Nepal, Niger, Nicaragua, or Micronesia, there are commonalities that all RPCVs share and there is always a welcome audience to hear more Peace Corps stories wherever RPCVs gather.

RPCVs advocate for Congressional funding and support for the Peace Corps. What RPCVs do not tend to do is speak with a powerful voice on issues of national or international importance. In recognition of the need, NPCA facilitated the creation of cause-focused affiliate groups like PC Association for Iran, RPCVs for Environmental Action, and PC Community for Refugees, but more can be done.

The other voices that come through loud and clear on issues of critical national importance often push agendas of self-interest rather than common interest. In my opinion, this is another immense missed opportunity. Thanks to Peace Corps service, we had the opportunity to view our country through foreign eyes, gaining a valuable alternative perspective. We were able to observe systems in other countries that performed better than our own in some areas and observe dysfunctional systems that helped us understand what we need to safeguard at home.

Assuming that the ideals that led us to the Peace Corps remain intact, we are a counterbalance for self-interest lobbying groups. We avoid taking a stand on important issues from a need to be bipartisan, recognizing that RPCVs elect representatives on both sides of the aisle. In large part, we do not speak out with a united voice because we have bought into the idea that issues like voting rights, immigration, criminal justice reform, environmental protection, tax reform, and education are partisan issues. I believe this is misguided. Who we support for public office *is* partisan, and any group representing RPCVs is wise to avoid campaigning for particular candidates. The issues themselves are not partisan and should be open to robust debate.

Bi-Partisan Nature of Peace Corps

There are RPCV groups focused on environmental protection and refugees who could lead the way in these two areas. Another affiliate group, Global Allies Program/RESULTS, makes it easy for RPCVs to positively impact global health, education, and other development issues affecting the developing world. RESULTS lobbies annually for legislation to create a more just and equitable world, both in the U.S. and internationally. RESULTS does all the legwork, provides the backup data, and prepares draft messages to send to members of Congress. RESULTS could be even more effective if there were coordinated support from the entire RPCV community, RESULTS could conceivably assist other affiliate groups to increase their reach and amplify Peace Corps values.

Individual RPCVs in positions of influence draw on their Peace Corps experiences, with the values they learned through their service informing their work. Diplomats like Ambassador Gina Abercrombie-Winstanley, Secretary of Health and Human Services Donna Shalala, members of Congress like Sam Farr, John Garamendi, and Joe Kennedy, Senator Chris Dodd, journalists Chris Matthews and Maureen Orth, NASA astronauts Mae Jemison and Joe Acaba, Levi Strauss & Co. CEO Emeritus Bob Haas, and Netflix Founder & CEO Reed Hastings would surely have achieved great success with or without Peace Corps service, but their Peace Corps values were evident in how they exercised their power and influence – mostly as individuals in their individual spheres.

Contributions by Returned Peace Corps Volunteers

Numerous people have returned from Peace Corps service to create social impact organizations and enterprises that serve the developing world with health clinics, education programs, refugee assistance programs, and even volunteer experiences for Africans. As philanthropists, RPCVs are among the most generous contributors to local, national, and international humanitarian efforts, volunteer activities, and activism, but they tend to engage individually, not as a united force for good.

At its height, NPCA represented over 185 affiliate groups of RPCVs living in various regions across the United States, RPCVs who had served in over 80 different countries, and RPCVs representing interest areas such as environment, LGBTQ+, refugee assistance, etc. Perhaps it is the independent nature of people who served in the Peace Corps, but we tend to remain in our silos, resisting attempts to form a cohesive front, except in the very limited lobbying sphere to promote and protect the Peace Corps. Still, only a small fraction of RPCVs advocate their elected officials, and with marginal impact. In 2022, even that broke down, as a vocal minority challenged the existence of both NPCA and the Peace Corps. Granted, both organizations could be better, but I am convinced the world is a better place owing to the existence of the National Peace Corps Association (NPCA), its affiliate group network, and the Peace Corps.

Disruptive Change in NPCA Leadership

The abrupt, reckless, and disruptive dismissal of NPCA President and CEO Glenn Blumhorst – considered by many to be the most consequential leader in the history of the organization – in June of 2022 resulted in leadership and funding vacuums that represent an existential threat to NPCA. Blumhorst had led NPCA's historic transformation from a struggling alumni association to a dynamic impact organization, focusing resources on amplifying the collective voice and global social impact of the Peace Corps community by enabling, empowering, and promoting RPCV groups and enterprises.

It remains to be seen if NPCA can recover or if another organization will emerge to unite RPCVs and amplify our voices, but a modern and professional governance structure would be needed to avoid repeated catastrophes in the future. The recently established 501(c)(3) Peace Corps Foundation, led by a board of former Peace Corps directors, former members of Congress, and successful business leaders, seems well-suited to this role.

The potential is there, and at times, we have achieved greatness. In 2000, five RPCVs successfully facilitated negotiations to end the border war between Eritrea and Ethiopia, which was possible because both sides in the conflict respected and trusted RPCVs. The government of Colombia bestowed honorary citizenship on RPCV Maureen Orth for championing quality education for impoverished youth in Colombia.

Greatness is also achieved in small arenas. Ask the indigenous people who now receive quality health care in their own language after Brian Goff-Smith returned, as promised, to work with them to establish a clinic for Alta Vera Paz, Guatemala. RPCV Sandra Del Prado and her husband, Guido, work with the indigenous community to provide affordable and accessible health care at the Kausay Wasi Clinic in Coya, Peru. Haitian Education and Leadership Program in Haiti, Corps Africa Volunteers, and Educate Tomorrow's program for former foster youth – all grew out of the Peace Corps experience, and all provide greater opportunities for people who are at the decision-making table, for possibly the first time. While it is true that money is essential, all stakeholders must be represented if the money is to be wisely spent. Great projects are possible when we recognize and respect the abilities and include the voices of the people we work with.

RPCVs as Goodwill Ambassadors

Respect goes a long way in building goodwill. International goodwill is intangible and priceless, and RPCVs bring it home as no one else does. At the Miami International Book Fair, first-generation Americans often stopped at our Returned Peace Corps Volunteer booth to inquire or reminisce about their volunteer, who had taught them in school or inspired them. When then Peace Corps Director Carrie Hessler-Radelet visited Sierra Leone, the President told her that if he ever came to the United States, he wanted her to reunite him with Sharon, the Peace Corps Volunteer who had inspired him as a young boy. Director Hessler-Radelet promised to do that.

When Sharon Alvarado got the call, she said she did not know the President of Sierra Leone, oblivious to what had become of the boy next door. Peace Corps Volunteers, who leave after two years, usually have little opportunity to view the ripple effects of their service. One RPCV, upon visiting a small town in Peru, was astounded at the number of people who stood in line to shake his hand because they fondly remembered a different volunteer who had once served in their community. Even 30 years later, we have the capacity to serve as goodwill ambassadors abroad, and we are equally poised to represent our second country at home.

After the September 11th attacks, RPCVs from Muslim countries spoke out forcefully to remind people we were attacked by individuals who did not represent the Muslim religion any more than the Ku Klux Klan represents Christianity. Unfortunately, it often takes a tragedy to get people to think about things that do not affect them directly, but we can make a conscious effort in our daily lives to find opportunities to build small bridges of understanding.

It troubles me when people harshly criticize other nations for not appreciating U.S. generosity. Arguing doesn't usually change minds, but if we consciously set out to share stories with a different narrative, we may move the needle. I, for one, should share the story more frequently of my evacuation from Albania, when the Albanian Peace Corps staff stayed with us until the last PCV was safely on a helicopter out while their own families and homes and country were engulfed in chaos. Since the U.S. Embassy had already closed, they had little hope of receiving their next paycheck anytime soon (they did get them, eventually). They stayed with us for myriad reasons, none of which suggest any lack of appreciation for the U.S. and its people.

PCVs have a host of memories of small kindnesses and generosity we experienced from people in our host countries. If we all make a point to share those stories whenever possible, it will go a long way toward achieving the third goal of the Peace Corps, "To help promote a better understanding of other peoples on the part of Americans."

Relationships Based on Trust and Respect

Peace Corps relationships tend to be based on trust and respect, as are all healthy relationships. When we started The Colombia Project in early 2000, I was highly motivated by memories of the warm hospitality I had received 30 years earlier. I was deeply troubled by the violence and displacement in Colombia at the time and eager to do anything I could to ease the pain in a country that had been so kind to me.

Conor Bohan started the Haitian Education and Leadership Program because he was inspired by a young woman whose talents and dreams to become a doctor were almost dashed for lack of a few thousand dollars.

Liz Fanning started Corps Africa in response to the laments of young Africans who wished they could have a Peace Corps-type experience. More than 400 African volunteers have worked on 800 projects in six African countries thanks to Corps Africa and experienced the joy of service.

How can we encourage more programs to build on the Peace Corps experience? Senator Chris Dodd, who served in the Dominican Republic as a young Peace Corps Volunteer, advocates that we "Set aside a portion of the annual Peace Corps budget as seed monies; the funds could go to active volunteers for demonstration projects at their sites and for returned volunteers interested in 'third goal' projects at home."

RPCVs vs. PCVs

I think Senator Dodd was on target regarding what is needed, but he missed the mark on who should provide it and who would pay for it. I would provide seed money and technical assistance for projects by RPCVs rather than PCVs. In my experience with TCP Global, I see a much higher quality of work from those with a full two years of Peace Corps experience under their belts. PCVs are still on the steep upward climb of the learning curve. Nor do I think the Peace Corps is well suited to promote innovation. The Peace Corps has become a risk-averse, top-heavy bureaucracy in order to survive for 62 years. While it still provides a quality experience for its volunteers and builds bridges of understanding, it no longer shows the innovation and energy of the heady Sargent Shriver days. RPCVs are a better bet.

It's been said that the Peace Corps experience is equivalent to getting a master's degree worth of knowledge, and RPCVs are ready to put that experience to good use and can hit the ground running to get things done. A glance at the list of impressive RPCV projects that received the John F. Kennedy, Sargent Shriver, Loret Miller Ruppe, Franklin H. Williams and Lillian Carter awards over the years is just the tip of the iceberg of the impressive contributions made by RPCVs, long after they completed their service.

They have done it largely on their own by serving the small and remote communities that development experts and major funders recognize as the most in need of assistance and the most overlooked.

Peace Corps Presence in Small and Remote Communities

According to a 2001 study released by the International Monetary Fund: "Rural poverty accounts for nearly 63% of poverty worldwide, reaching 90% in some countries like Bangladesh and between 65 and 90% in sub-Saharan Africa."[70]

The importance of investing in small and remote communities has its own chapter in this book, but it is important to mention it here, as well. Most Peace Corps Volunteers serve in small and remote communities, and many remain connected to those communities well after their service ends. Brian Goff Smith completed four years of Peace Corps service in Alta Vera Paz, Guatemala, in 2006, returned to the U.S. to earn a medical degree, and then returned to Guatemala, as promised, to build a clinic where he still spends part of each year. Twenty-five years after completing their Peace Corps service, Virginia Emmons and Jocelyn Farrington remain involved in collaborative and impactful service in their rural Niger villages.

When these RPCVs contribute to improving the lot of people in communities they care about, they are also contributing to making migration a choice rather than a necessity. By helping people to improve their quality of life, providing economic resources, access to educational opportunities, and health care, they make it easier for people to remain in their community of birth if they so choose, thereby reducing stress on cities ill-equipped to accommodate an influx of rural migrants.

The world's largest humanitarian network, the International Red Cross and Red Crescent Societies (IFRC) released a World Disasters Report in 2018 that noted: "Donors should consider

70 Mahmood Hasan Khan, "Rural Poverty in Developing Countries," Finance and Development - a quarterly magazine of the IMF, Volume 37, no 4 (December, 2000) https://www.imf.org/external/pubs/ft/fandd/2000/12/khan.htm.

funding that promotes programming that reaches the people most in need, even if they are the hardest to reach … International organizations need to invest in the people most able to be present and to provide services in the hardest-to-reach areas, including local actors and communities themselves."[71]

I suggest that among "the people most able to be present and to provide services in the hardest-to-reach areas," we should include Virginia, Jocelyn, Brian and other RPCVs linked to such communities. TCP Global partners with grassroots organizations in more than 100 remote villages. Former Peace Corps language instructor Yogi Kayastha sometimes walks more than a day to reach remote sites in Nepal to provide oversight to community-based organizations helping people improve their quality of life.

Few Resources for Local Change-Makers

TCP Global and P2P, two organizations founded and led by RPCVs, partner with local leaders in the Yumbe District of Northern Uganda, an area so remote that the Peace Corps doesn't even go there. TCP Global empowered the local women through micro-loans and facilitated the formation of possibly the world's only Rotary Club established by market vendors and subsistence farmers. Together with P2P, they continue to support Rotarians' efforts to bring clean water, sanitation, and anti-malaria programs to poor villages. Priorities are set locally, and the people dig their own latrines and recently learned to dig their own wells. As they walk, ride their bikes, or hitch a ride on a moto to reach villages up to 20 kilometers outside of town, they are often left in the dust by the 4-wheel Drive vehicles of NGOs visiting the Bidibidi Refugee Camp. It is frustrating what few resources the Yumbe Rotarians have available.

At the very least, they could use international funding for a vehicle to facilitate visits to 40 loan sites and multiple villages targeted for improvements. They would adopt more villages for

---

71 World Disasters Report 2018, "Out of Reach: Remote and Hard to Access Locations," 82 https://www.ifrc.org/sites/default/files/2021-09/C-03-WDR-2018-3-reach.pdf.

improvement if they had $20,000 per village, but they don't need funding at the $1 million level and, therefore, are not attractive to major foundations. However, if the Peace Corps Foundation or some organization representing a broad spectrum of RPCVs could administer a major grant and reallocate those funds, many RPCV efforts could scale up, and others could start up.

A Little Goes a Long Way in the Right Hands

Two organizations could scale up quickly and significantly. TCP Global commits to $9,000 per site over a three-year period and is currently empowering women entrepreneurs through microloans in over 150 communities. We could easily double that number with adequate funding. P2P estimates $20,000 per village (assuming 500-700 residents) to provide a full array of water, sanitation, and health services to dramatically reduce preventable diseases like malaria, diarrhea, and dysentery. That $20,000 could buy wells to make water readily accessible, thus freeing girls to attend school; sufficient latrine covers and vents for every family to have a latrine, as required by law; hand-wash stations, water filters, malaria testing and treatment.

The 2018 World Disaster Report quoted above goes on to say: "Humanitarian organizations and donors need to prioritize filling gaps in assistance to the communities that are most neglected and hardest to reach."

The RPCV community could fill those gaps by directing resources to RPCVs partnering with grassroots service providers. Some RPCVs are former senators, representatives, university presidents, cabinet members, leaders of tech companies, and members of foundation boards who could connect the donors and the do-ers through the RPCV network – another missed opportunity.

In 2011 Sis Yamah asked PCV Charlene Espinoza (left) for help with a girls' club. They soon realized there was a market for the bags the girls produced. They created Bosh Bosh Inc.

In 2020, PCV Karlin Scudder made the connection to TCP Global and now virtually mentors the loan program.

Bosh Bosh provides free education and vocational training, preparing the next generation for a better future. Beyond making beautiful bags from locally sourced materials, it's about transferring skills and empowering girls and women through education.

BOSH BOSH - a Peace Corps Story ... Nov 17, 2022

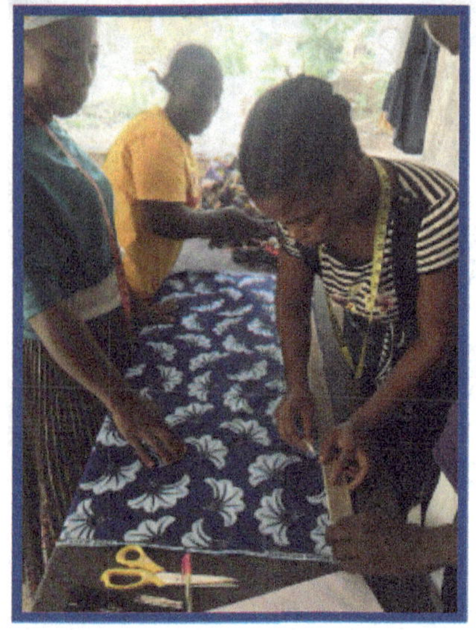

About Us What we do Online Boutique Meet the Team Products Get Involved Donate Blog Contact

Bosh Bosh was established by Charlene Espinoza when she was a Peace Corps Volunteer (PCV) in Salala, Liberia in 2011. In 2020, Liberia PCV Karlin Scudder connected Bosh Bosh to TCP Global.

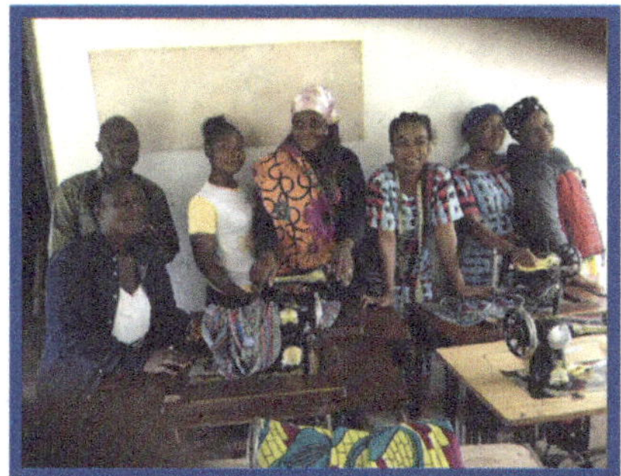

These Gbarnga women say that 'Knowledge is Power" and therefore they want to continue sewing classes with Bosh Bosh. They are working to build a better future and are grateful to TCP Global for opening doors for them.

CHAPTER 12

PRACTICAL MICRO-LOANS: THE TCP GLOBAL MODEL

"My hope for the future is that we learn wisdom again."
Jane Goodall, anthropologist and United Nations Messenger for Peace

The most important rule is to "First do no harm." The road to hell is paved with good intentions. Good intentions may be enough to make us feel good, but unless we proceed thoughtfully, we run the risk of creating dependency, luring people off their frugal and sustainable path into unsustainable behaviors, undermining local initiatives, and creating division within a community. Even when we do our due diligence, there is no 100% guarantee that we will avoid these pitfalls, but we can minimize the risk.

Finding the right partners is the key to working effectively from afar in small villages. It is also the most difficult challenge. For the first 20 years, The Colombia Project-TCP Global struggled to find good partners. Our model is simple, but it is sufficiently different from other loan programs that the people we aspire to serve have a difficult time understanding how we work. There is natural skepticism about new programs because grassroots organizations have wasted countless time and energy in the past, pursuing empty promises by those who came before us and offered to help. They have every reason to believe we could be more of the same.

TCP Global Supports the Primary Mission of Partner Organizations

Our initial plan was to find organizations working successfully in marginalized communities in the health, education, empowerment, or environmental sectors and then provide them funds to set up affordable small-loan programs for their clients. Rather than a distraction, TCP Global empowers the organization and its clients to achieve its primary mission better. The organization may use loan program earnings to further its primary mission: provide a library, science lab or computers for their school; provide a latrine as one partner did in Guatemala so that pregnant ladies could get the full range of health screenings; provide exercise equipment for physically-challenged people as several partners did in Colombia.

As their clients increase their earnings through small business loans, they become better able to achieve the non-profit's environmental, health or educational goals. If the loan program is successful, TCP Global will continue to send funds for their permanent loan pool until they have sufficient resources to meet the micro-loan needs of the community. We do not want to overwhelm the grassroots partner or undermine their primary mission and, therefore, recommended no more than 30-40 open loans.

In the first seven years, we found two partners through a network of Returned Peace Corps Volunteers who had served in Colombia and one through a young Colombian woman who stayed at my house through an exchange program sponsored by the League of Women Voters. It was pretty much like looking for needles in the proverbial haystack.

Initial Resistance and Then Success

In the early years in Colombia, we had unsuccessfully pursued a collaboration with MINICOL, an organization of expat Colombians providing education and mentoring for impoverished children in rural Colombia. They said our loans were too small, the project too time-consuming, and they dismissed our overtures.

That all changed when my daughter died in 2006, and her best friend from fifth grade, who was by then a doctor, invited me to lunch. Her parents were Colombian, and my daughter, Ashley, had once told her friend, Nora, that I ran a loan program in Colombia. Nora asked me about it over lunch and then convinced her parents, who were on the MINICOL board, to give our program a try.

Over the next few years, we opened MINICOL loan programs in multiple small towns. The most successful, SONCOL in La Victoria, has issued 656 loans worth $189,445 to date, investing each dollar we sent nine times. SONCOL has used $28,000 of its $33,000 in earnings for facility repairs, COVID relief, higher education for its graduates, and a women's sewing cooperative. Multiple MINICOL sites thrived for two to ten years until staff changes or COVID made it impossible for them to continue. It took a major tragedy to bring forth what turned out to be a valuable connection. Through 2019, it remained a challenge to find good partners.

COVID Evacuations in 2020 Changed Everything

When 7300 Peace Corps Volunteers were hastily evacuated due to the COVID pandemic in March of 2020, many of them searched for ways to continue to be of service. Several coordinated by email with their old Peace Corps sites to open TCP Global loan programs. A chance encounter at a March 2020 event for Returned Peace Corps Volunteers in Washington opened the floodgates for new sites. After adding 71 in 2021, we had to change strategies in order to control growth.

As of 2023, finding new, effective partners is no longer challenging for TCP Global. Keeping up with the demand is now the issue. Since each new site involves a potential commitment of $9000, the seventy-one sites added in 2021 represented a potential outlay of $639,000 and caused us to change how new sites are admitted. As of November 2021, new sites must find the first $1500, reducing the TCP Global potential commitment to $7500 per site. Still, nearly fifty sites were added in 2022, and we struggle to meet our commitments to our partners.

Not all sites make it to graduation. Several sites were closed when we discovered they were charging 15% monthly interest, which they said was typical for Micro-Finance Institutions. That violates our written agreement, and although one of those sites offered to reduce their interest, TCP Global will not work with partners that do not have the best interest of their clients as the top priority. If they were willing to charge 15% monthly interest, we could no longer trust their judgment. Another closed when a due-diligence visit confirmed suspicions that the program supported church projects rather than entrepreneurial loans.

Several partners did good work, but their program models resulted in loan funds sitting idle for long periods. Others failed to send reports or fell significantly below our 95% good repayment rate requirement. More than 100 sites appear to be on the path to success, and 64 have graduated as of April 2023 as fully funded and operating sustainably.

Since 2000, The Colombia Project / TCP Global has been run by volunteers, with virtually no overhead in the U.S., allowing 100% of donations to be distributed as micro-loans in marginalized communities worldwide. When the National Peace Corps Association served as a fiscal sponsor from 2016 to 2022, we maintained a separate funding stream to cover their 15% fee. When TCP Global became a 501(c)3 in 2023, we adopted a new policy, allowing up to 10% of donations for overhead unless specifically prohibited by a donor.

The TCP Global model is simple, but it took us more than seven years, while we still operated as The Colombia Project, to figure it out.

1. TCP GLOBAL MODEL

A. Partner Requirements

- Recommended by a trusted source
- Registered in the country where they work
- Bank account in the name of the organization
- Already working effectively to serve a marginalized community

- Has an existing program in health, environment, empowerment, education, etc.
- As of 2020, Women's Village Savings and Loan Associations (VSLAs) with at least one year of loan experience may partner with TCP Global through a fiscal agent meeting the above requirements.

B. Benefits to TCP Global of a partner already working in the community

- A grassroots organization that prioritizes community service is likely to continue providing effective service once they partner with TCP Global. Thus, we can put our trust in them.
- Since they know the community, they are in a good position to vet loan applicants.
- Since they already have salaries, rent and utilities covered, other than loan funds, start-up costs are negligible.
- Being well-respected in the community, the likelihood of repayment on their loans is high.

C. Benefits to partner from working with TCP Global

- As the loans empower clients to improve household income, they can better achieve the education, environmental, health, etc. goals of the partnering nonprofit.
- Earnings from TCP Global give the partner a permanent funding stream to support community projects.

D. Responsibilities documented in a written agreement

- Partners will only issue loans for revenue-generating activities to unbanked, impoverished entrepreneurs.
- Partners will charge interest (or a fee in Muslim countries) that shall not exceed the local bank rates.
- Partner will submit regular reports of loan activity.
- Partner will keep TCP Global funds fully invested in viable loans. This ensures that the maximum number of people

benefit. It also decreases opportunities for theft. If funds are invested in borrowers, there are no funds in the office to steal.

- Partner will provide the first $1,500 to start the program. This requirement was added in November 2021 after our success was well documented.
- Partner has the right to all interest collected on the loans plus 50% of funds sent AFTER they have been invested twice. ($9,000 sent in total = $4,500 for the partner and $4,500 in the permanent, revolving loan pool.)
- TCP Global will provide an additional $1,500 allocation after all previous funds have been invested twice if the reports confirm a repayment rate of at least 95%.
- If available, TCP Global will continue sending funds based on good reports until the loan program has sufficient funds to support local demand. Typically, this means a loan pool capable of supporting two loans of $300 to each borrower each year.

E. Reporting

- TCP Global will provide a Daily Log in the local language for each new site.
- Partner submits reports regularly to update data for that site and, in return, will receive a Site Summary Report, which they can use to verify that TCP Global records agree with their records.
- The daily log also updates a Global Summary Report that converts the local currency to dollars (using the exchange rate at which those dollars entered the program) and provides data on average loan amounts, delinquency, earnings, interest rate, open loans, etc., allowing for comparison of performance across countries and sites.
- Reporting requirements are kept to a minimum. Sites enter the borrower's name, date and either the new loan amount or the payment amount. They also note in the log when they withdraw earnings or receive new funds.

F. Modifications to accommodate VSLAs with no bank account

- Identify an appropriate fiscal agent nonprofit to work with the VSLAs.
- Modify the agreement to refer to multiple VSLA loan sites
- Create an agreement with the fiscal agent
- Typically, the VSLA receives interest income, while the fiscal agent receives the 50% earnings
- The fiscal agent disburses 100% of funds received to VSLA
- The fiscal agent sends reports.
- VSLAs must already have one year of experience managing a loan program from their combined savings.
- Encourage networking of VSLAs to support each other

G. Sustainability

- Within five years, each loan site is expected to become self-sustaining, with sufficient funds to meet the micro-loan needs of the community.
- The loan pool should be managed by an entity that is a permanent part of the community.
- With the very first funding allocations, the loan program is sustainable. Even if TCP Global ceased to exist and no further funds were sent, the partner could continue to recycle the funds already received.
- Borrowers are encouraged to progress to bank loans to continue climbing the ladder of economic success, making room for new borrowers needing small loans.

H. Flexibility

- Partners have maximum flexibility to make the program work well in their situation.
- Partners set loan terms, interest rates, number and frequency of payments.

- Partners define the application and approval processes.
- The mission of TCP Global is to empower marginalized entrepreneurs with affordable loans. We consider reasonable requests from partners who plan to achieve that mission in a way that differs from the usual process.

Nepal Adaptations

In Nepal, TCP Global works with partners funded by the Development Fund Norway (DFN) that provide animal husbandry and agriculture training to help people in remote, mountainous settlements earn a decent living at home. Some borrowers are a two-day walk from the nearest roads. While most partners file monthly reports for borrowers who make monthly payments on short-term loans, in Nepal, borrowers make one payment at the end of a six to eight-month cycle, and reports on that activity come at eight to ten-month intervals. Since TCP Global loans complement DFN training, allowing Nepalese to implement what they learn from DFN, we accommodate their alternative reporting arrangement.

Yogi Kayastha, a former Peace Corps language instructor, is the DFN country coordinator for Nepal and makes periodic visits to the sites. DFN-TCP Global support proved particularly important when tourism in Nepal ceased and migrant workers returned from India during the COVID pandemic.

TCP Global & P2P & Rotarians
Development through local change-makers

STEP ONE: RELIEF FROM ABJECT POVERTY

"TCP Global fund ...benefited 1,060 women directly and over 5000 families indirectly and has seen the beneficiary groups improve on their business and lives in general. The beneficiaries are now capable of paying school fees for their children. All in all, the general impact of TCP program in Yumbe is ultimate reduction in the poverty level among the rural women and their communities." *Innocent Ajaga - CCEDUC - Yumbe, Uganda*

TCP Global Newsletter of October 6, 2022

Small loans of $50 to $300 allow entrepreneurs to improve their businesses and increase income so they can better feed, house, and educate their families.

Given adequate resources they know how to care for their families.

Borrowers often start with 2-3 goats, and quickly expand to increase economic security.

HOW THE TCP GLOBAL MODEL IS DIFFERENT

Instead of money for salary and infrastructure, our money goes directly to change makers in the community.

TCP Global Newsletter of October 6, 2022

STEP TWO: STOP PREVENTABLE ILLNESSES

If people are too sick to go to work, or spend much of their earnings curing illnesses, economic progress is not possible.

Chris Roesel, TCP Global's Director for Africa programs, applies knowledge gained through 40 years of field experience to help TCP Global partners improve health outcomes.

Chris established People to People (P2P) to provide mentoring and funds for water, sanitation and health programs.

TCP Global and P2P work together to remove obstacles to economic development.

TCP Global Newsletter of October 6, 2022

Yumbe Rotarians, supported by P2P, adopted Achiba Village to provide low-tech hand-wash stations and latrines, health workshops, and a new bore hole for improved access to water.

They achieved dramatic results as the following survey indicates.

:	8-11-21	7-27-22
Get water from protected source	13%	100%
Have access to latrine	35%	100%
Have access to hand washing facility	10%	100%
Children < 5 with diarrhea in last 2 weeks	50%	5%
Income spent on diarrhea treatment	11%	3%
Diagnosed with malaria	75%	36%

v

Yumbe Rotarians recruiting applications for the next village to adopt.

TCP Global Newsletter of October 6, 2022

STEP 3: COMMUNITY EMPOWERMENT

Rotarians engaged community leaders in Achiba to promote education for girls, teach hygiene, plant trees and to set up water committees to maintain the bore holes.

Rotarians work with villagers to keep the latrines, bore holes and hand wash stations clean.

TCP Global Newsletter of October 6, 2022

CHAPTER 13

AVOIDING MORAL BANKRUPTCY

> "When morality comes up against profit, it is seldom that profit loses."
> *Shirley Chisholm, the first African-American woman elected to serve in the U.S. Congress*

WHAT IF we wrested our country back from the control of corporate interests with their outsized influence?

What IF we reversed Citizens United or legislated it out of existence?

What IF politicians were made to be responsive to the wishes, or at least the best interests of their constituents, rather than self-interest groups?

Farm Policy as an Example

"Our food system is broken, but it didn't get that way by accident. The food on our plates has been shaped by a misguided series of pro-corporate policies that carve out an agricultural system that works for the few at the expense of the many. Farm policy — combined with growing corporate consolidation and unchecked power — siphons money away from family farmers and the communities that depend on them and supports industrial farming systems that harm our soil and water, communities, economies and health."[72]

Policies enacted by politicians, heavily dependent on corporate donations, wreak havoc beyond our borders as well.

> "Mexico: The Cost of U.S. Dumping: For years, developing countries have complained that rich countries undermine their agricultural development by 'dumping' surplus commodities on them—that is, by exporting their grains and other products at prices below what it cost to produce them. But how much does such dumping cost farmers in developing countries? According to my new study of U.S. dumping on Mexico after NAFTA, Mexican farmers, on average, lost more than $1 billion per year during the nine-year period of 1997–2005, with more than half the losses suffered by the country's embattled corn farmers."[73]

Farmers cannot compete with the cheap, subsidized U.S. produce. Farmers undercut by subsidized U.S. products have no earnings to use to plant crops the following year and are often put out of business, with few options other than to join the throngs of people at our borders. The problem identified above in 2006 continues and only grows worse.

An article titled "NAFTA an empty basket for farmers in southern Mexico," published in September 2014 by Cronkite Borderlands Project, reports that: "As U.S. farmers exported their subsidized corn to Mexico, local producer prices plummeted, and small farmers could no longer earn enough to live on. Rural farmers left Southern Mexico in droves and migrated north, spurring increasing numbers of undocumented immigrants to the U.S. from Southern Mexico states."[74]

Little has changed in the eight years since the Cronkite ASU article was published. According to a 2022 Opinion piece in The

72 https://www.farmaid.org/category/issues/farm-policy/.

73 #https://nacla.org/news/mexico-cost-us-dumping

74 https://cronkite.asu.edu/projects/buffett/chiapas/nafta-an-empty-basket-for-farmers-in-southern-mexico/#:~:text=As%20U.S.%20farmers%20exported%20their%20subsidized%20corn%20to,immigrants%20to%20the%20U.S.%20from%20Southern%20Mexico%20states

Hill, "My organization, the Institute for Agriculture and Trade Policy (IATP), has calculated the rates of dumping for corn, wheat, rice, soy and cotton since the 1990s. During NAFTA's first decade, corn was exported at an average of 15% below the cost of production. As of 2017, dumping rates were 9% for corn, 38% for wheat and 3% for rice. …"[75]

Thanks to subsidies, U.S. produce was sold overseas at less than what it cost to grow the crops. Small wonder that Mexican farmers cannot compete. Small wonder so many are driven to cross the border into the U.S.

The Hill article continues, "According to census data calculations by researchers at the Mexican Centro de Investigación y Docencia Económicas, some 4.9 million Mexican family farmers were displaced after NAFTA, with about 3 million becoming seasonal workers in agro-export industries. This shift was part of a dramatic reconfiguration of supply chains and a sharp increase in corporate concentration in agriculture in North America, as global firms shifted different stages of production among countries to reduce costs. Production of feed corn by ever larger farmers in Mexico expanded alongside corn imports from the U.S., contributing to the vicious cycle of farm loss and corporate concentration that has hurt farmers in both countries."[76]

Small loans from TCP Global can serve as "Band-Aids" to help individual farmers adjust to market changes, but microcredit is no substitute for the macroeconomic changes needed to solve the problem. It is easier for our representatives to do the right thing when they hear encouragement from their constituents. There are always self-interest groups knocking on lawmakers' doors. We need to make sure they hear from concerned citizens, as well.

WHAT IF we took the time to express our opinion to elected officials each time they did something that appalled or enthralled us?

---

75 Karen Hansen-Kuhn, "Time for new approaches to US-Mexico corn trade." The Hill, November 3, 2022

76 https://thehill.com/opinion/international/3718625-time-for-new-approaches-to-us-mexico-corn-trade/

WHAT IF we sought to end the chaos at the Southern border by getting to the root cause and amending U.S. farm policy rather than enhancing border security?

The farm policy is hardly an anomaly. As Robert Reich, former secretary of Health and Human Services in the Clinton administration wrote in an August 21, 2022, article published in The Guardian,

> "America used to regulate business. Now government subsidizes it. From 1932 through the late 1970s, the government mainly regulated businesses. This was the era of the alphabet soup of regulatory agencies begun under Franklin D. Roosevelt (the SEC, ICC, FCC, CAB, and so on), culminating in the EPA of 1970.
>
> The government still regulates businesses, of course, but the biggest thing the federal government now does with businesses is subsidize them....
>
> In truth, the three-decades-long shift in power to big corporations has transformed industrial policy into a system for bribing them to do the sorts of things government once demanded they do as the price for being part of the American system."[77]

According to the Center for Economic Accountability (CEA), 2022 was apparently the worst year ever for corporate subsidies, which does not bode well for 2023 and 2024:

> "Facing election-year pressure from voters and flush with federal cash, governors across America have signed three times more billion-dollar subsidy deals than any previous year in history.
>
> September 15, 2022 – An unprecedented flood of economic development 'megadeals' with potential billion-dollar price

---

77 Robert Reich, America used to regulate business. Now government subsidises it, *The Guardian*, August 21, 2022, https://www.theguardian.com/commentisfree/2022/aug/21/america-used-to-regulate-business-now-government-subsidises-it

tags across the United States is turning 2022 into a uniquely expensive year for corporate welfare at the state and local level. Across the country and on both sides of the partisan divide, state governments have crammed a decade's worth of billion-dollar subsidy deals into less than a single year.

America's governors and mayors are shoveling billion-dollar corporate welfare megadeals out the door this year at a rate that would normally take them a decade or more to achieve,' said John C. Mozena, president of the CEA. 'Under pressure from constituents to *do something* about the economy and with their budgets deceptively flush with one-time federal dollars, they're making short-sighted but big-ticket decisions that will be imposing massive costs on our communities for decades to come.

A Political Perfect Storm Drives the Mega Deal Stampede

America's economy may be in a state of disruption, but the evidence is that the unprecedented pace of billion-dollar deals in 2022 is driven more by the political response to the economy than by actual economic best practices.

These deals fly in the face of a broad consensus among economists and independent experts that economic development subsidies rarely change corporate decision-making and have little – if any – impact on employment rates or other measures of economic well-being.

Where they do generate measurable value, however, is for politicians facing an election. The evidence has been clear for some time that economic development subsidies are much better political tools for the politicians who hand them out than they are economic tools for the communities they're supposed to improve. It's the fundamental truth of economic development subsidies: They don't exist to create jobs as much as they do to make voters believe that politicians are responsible for creating jobs.

Independent research supports the political roots of economic development subsidies. Studies have found that states where governors are running for reelection, are more than twice as likely as those where they are not to see a sudden large increase in subsidy spending; that governors can move independent voter intent by as much as 9% by 'winning' 1,000 manufacturing jobs with subsidies and that elected officials who make subsidy deals receive more in political donations and have larger margins of victory on Election Day as those who don't."[78]

Corporate Welfare Gets a Pass

In the midterm elections of 2022, Republicans in Florida overcame a nationwide blue wave by creating fear that "socialism" was undermining our way of life, but without even a passing reference to corporate welfare disguised as subsidies.

As Robert Reich explains, the whole relationship between corporations and government has been turned on its head. One goal of governments, as I was taught, was to create a level playing field where every person and every business had the opportunity to go as far as their talent, initiative and energy would take them. Regulations ensured no one gained an unfair advantage by exploiting workers, damaging the environment, or undermining a fair system.

Thanks to Citizens United, we now have a system in which moneyed interests have usurped power from the people to make the government serve the interest of campaign donors instead of the country's interests. Thus, rather than regulations, we have subsidies for Big Oil, Big Pharma, Big Ag and other special interests so they can eliminate competition and exploit both the environment and their workers to accumulate even more wealth. It is up to voters to let elected representatives know where we stand.

WHAT IF we more accurately identified corporate subsidies as corporate welfare and subjected corporate welfare to the same scrutiny applied to subsidies for our citizens?

---

78 "2022 Is the Worst Year in History for State Corporate Welfare Megadeals," Center for Economic Accountability,https://economicaccountability.org/2022/09/15/2022-is-the-worst-year-in-history-for-state-corporate-welfare-megadeals/.

While many industries receive government subsidies, three of the biggest beneficiaries are energy, agriculture, and transportation. The Environmental and Energy Study Institute found that the U.S. government alone spends $20 billion every year on direct fossil fuel subsidies. Of that figure, around $16 billion goes toward oil and gas, while the remaining $4 billion benefits the coal industry. This despite almost universal agreement that fossil fuels threaten life on the planet.[79]

Meanwhile, the Wall Street Journal reported that, in 2017, six oil company executives earned more than $20 million in annual salary and perks. While gas prices were rising in 2021, "On average, each CEO made $1.6 million more last year than they did in 2020. The bonuses for 14 CEOs alone totaled $31.8 million."[80] One thing these CEOs likely did to earn those big increases was to keep the oil subsidies in place.

WHAT IF we stopped subsidizing things that are bad for the planet and regulated those industries instead? That would require changing campaign finance laws to make politicians responsive again to the people rather than to corporate interests.

WHAT IF we eliminated double standards and made corporations and their CEOs responsible for the long-term impacts of their actions? Rather than taxpayers covering the bill to clean up toxic dumps and spills, healthcare for those addicted to opioids, and subsidies for workers who are not paid a living wage, why not establish an escrow account for the oil, coal, pharmaceutical, sugar, chemical, industries etc., to cover all damages and lawsuits resulting from their industry and let them police their own members, to assign liability, accordingly. It is not realistic for the government to police a highly specialized industry when all the brightest minds in that industry are working for the companies and focused on

79 Johannes Urpelainen, Elisha George, "Reforming global fossil fuel subsidies: How the United States can restart international cooperation." Brookings Institute, July 14, 2021 https://www.brookings.edu/research/reforming-global-fossil-fuel-subsidies-how-the-united-states-can-restart-international-coop

80 https://truthout.org/articles/as-gas-prices-soared-in-2021-big-oil-ceos-got-a-nearly-45-million-raise/

ways to minimize liability and when our legislators are beholden to those industries.

WHAT IF the weapons industry was proportionally taxed one million dollars for each person killed by military-grade weapons rather than asking schoolchildren, shoppers, and moviegoers to bear the costs alone of keeping corporate profits high?

WHAT IF we recognized the unfair advantage realized from slave labor that disproportionately enriched U.S. institutions and corporations and deprived others of the opportunity to accumulate wealth from their own labor?

Slavery and the Catholic Church

St. Louis University (SLU), my alma mater, was built with money from the sale of Georgetown University slaves and benefitted from slave labor. In 2016, SLU joined "...an initiative to confront a joint history of involvement in the enslavement of African Americans that dates back to the founding of the university."[81] as reported in SLU's student newspaper, The University News. Intentions were good, but follow-through has been troubling.

According to the St. Louis Post Dispatch, "In 2021, the Jesuits vowed to raise $100 million for the foundation, with a longer-term goal of raising$1 billion to help reconcile with its history of slaveholding. But the foundation hasn't surpassed an initial $15 million donation from the Jesuits."[82]

The article reported, "A local partnership between the Jesuits and St. Louis University to research their history of slaveholding, including finding and reconciling with descendants, has been quietly downsized to a staff of one priest. The plan had been to

81 Conor Dorn, "Confronting SLU's History With Slavery." The University News, October 4, 2019.

82 Jesse Bogan, "Jesuit slaveholding history project downsized." St. Louis Post Dispatch, February 19, 2023, https://www.stltoday.com/jesuit-slaveholding-history-project-downsized/article_44f539f4-5087-5afd-9953-3b1b7e555048.html

invest in education for descendants and address racial problems in communities, but fundraising has fallen short."

This is a cause not likely to gain much support in my home state of Missouri, but there is another, richly endowed, and likely more receptive source of funding. A June 15, 2020, headline in the National Catholic Review proclaimed: "The Catholic Church must make reparation for its role in slavery."[83] The article goes on to state that "... at various moments in American history from the colonial era to the U.S. Civil War, the church was the largest corporate slaveholder in Florida, Louisiana, Maryland, Kentucky and Missouri…". Among the author's recommendations are "Reinvesting in and expanding the Black Catholic educational system; Requiring the teaching of Black and Brown Catholic history in every Catholic school and seminary; Endowing scholarships, fellowships and professorships for Black and Brown scholars at Catholic colleges and universities."

All roads have always led to Rome, where much of the ill-gotten wealth of the slave trade resides. This is a great opportunity for the Vatican to step up to the plate, sell off some of the worldly wealth it has accumulated and help Catholic institutions like St. Louis University do the right thing.

Vatican Treasures

When I first visited the Vatican, I was so repulsed by the garish display of worldly treasures that I raced through the Sistine Chapel and forgot to look up. Pope Francis made a giant step in the right direction in rescinding the Doctrine of Discovery, which justified colonialism and the exploitation of southern continents.

It is shameful that it took more than 500 years, during which a lot of wealth was drained from those continents that are today mired in poverty, while the Church and the colonial nations it empowered continue to enjoy their ill-gotten wealth. I hope Pope Francis lives

83 Shannen Dee Williams, "The Catholic Church must make reparations for its role in slavery." National Catholic Reporter, June 15, 2020, https://www.ncronline.org/vatican/vatican-news/pope-says-using-tinder-normal-talks-inclusivity-disney-documentary.

long enough to take the next step and make reparations by selling off Vatican treasures to invest heavily in equity for former colonies and slaves and investing, particularly in the African priests and nuns working to improve lives in former colonies.

Need for a Doctrine of Recovery

Despite its scandals, the Church has the potential to exercise considerable moral authority. I hope it does not miss this opportunity to lead by example by making amends for past moral failures with more than words. Poverty breeds violence. Without justice, there can be no peace. Greed has led the world down a dangerous path. A new *Doctrine of Recovery* could help people and countries recover what the Church empowered colonialists and slaveholders to take from them. Even the Pope has trouble getting the right things done without strong public support. Let's speak out and put pressure on Church leaders.

WHAT IF all institutions and families that profited from slavery, though unable to right the wrongs of the past, paid back-wages into a humanitarian services pool to mitigate the effects of those past injustices on descendants of slaves? This may curtail the lifestyle of slaveholder descendants, but that lifestyle has been unjustly enriched by the slave labor on which it was built. They have not earned *all* the riches they enjoy. Meanwhile, the slaves and their descendants suffered ongoing economic harm because they were not justly compensated for their labor and were thus deprived of the opportunity to accumulate wealth.

Reparations

While the sins of the father do not pass to the sons, there is also no justification for the wages of sin to pass to the sons. For descendants of slaveholders who are in the top one percent, it is reasonable to suggest that the present-day value of that slave labor that contributed to their wealth be reserved for scholarships, low-interest business loans, home subsidies and other programs to specifically benefit the descendants of people who suffered under slavery.

An August 29, 2019, article by Zoe Thomas of the BBC News notes that slaves built the wall that gave Wall Street its name and that a wide swath of U.S. businesses profited from the slave trade, including companies like New York Life, AIG, and Aetna, that "sold policies that insured slave owners would be compensated if the slaves they owned were injured or killed .... The predecessors that made up Citibank, Bank of America and Wells Fargo are among a list of well-known U.S. financial firms that benefitted from the slave trade."[84]

At the very least, those banks could be required to provide lower interest rates to descendants of former slaves. I was slow to join the bandwagon for reparations but have become a believer. I believe it is fair for those with enormous family fortunes built, at least in part, on any aspect of the slave trade to pay reparations commensurate with their slave trade profits.

WHAT IF France, the U.S., and any other countries that diverted Haiti's financial resources were compelled to allocate just a percentage of what they took and invest it in building Haiti's roads, electric grid, ports, airports, and water infrastructure, along with hospitals and schools? In the long run, we would all benefit from Haiti as a prosperous neighbor.

WHAT IF we recognized immigrants for the creative, innovative, determined risk-takers and tax-payers they are and stopped putting roadblocks in their path?

WHAT IF our elected representatives had to live with the consequences of the legislation they passed – no special health care and other perks for representatives?

WHAT IF white-collar crime were treated seriously? Corporate malfeasance does far more harm to individuals and society than a guy with a gun holding up a convenience store. There is the direct harm of any unfair practice they engage in, but that is surpassed by the damage resulting from destroying faith in the American system. Those of us who learn of corporate malfeasance through news articles quickly forget, but those who lose their health or loved

84 https://www.bbc.com/news/business-49476247.

ones in unsafe work environments, go to jail because a prosecutor suppressed exculpatory evidence, or fall victim to corporate scams, never forget. This is bad for them and society.

WHAT IF CEOs were held responsible for what happens on their watch? For most of us, big returns involve big risks. CEOs who control large corporations reap enormous profits with virtually no risk. Poorly performing CEOs receive generous severance packages, and their corporations are too often bailed out. Environmental degradation, healthcare scams, exploitive banking practices, and dangerous workplace practices conducted on their watch result in fines that are dwarfed by the profits realized from bad practices they failed to control and possibly encouraged – and no one goes to jail. At a minimum, CEOs should bear some personal financial responsibility for bad corporate behavior on their watch.

WHAT IF we recognized that white supremacy is more than white-robed people carrying torches? When Pope Francis visited Canada in 2022, he said, "Never again can the Christian community allow itself to be infected by the idea that one culture is superior to others, or that it is legitimate to employ ways of coercing others."[85]

An "All Things Considered" segment on NPR documented the deep ties between Southern Christianity and white supremacist ideologies.[86] "In 2020, the FBI and DHS assessed RMVEs [Racially Motivated Violent Extremist], primarily those advocating the superiority of the white race, likely would continue to be the most lethal category of the DT [Domestic Terrorist] threat to the Homeland."[87]

---

85 https://www.npr.org/2023/03/30/1167056438/vatican-doctrine-of-discovery-colonialism-indigenous

86 https://www.npr.org/2020/07/01/883115867/white-supremacist-ideas-have-historical-roots-in-u-s-christianity

87 "Strategic Intelligence Assessment and Data on Domestic Terrorism." Federal Bureau of Investigation Department of Homeland Security, (October 2022), 6. https://www.dni.gov/files/NCTC/documents/news_documents/2022_10_FBI-DHS_Strategic_Intelligence_Assessment_and_Data_on_Domestic_Terrorism.pdf.

Yet white-supremacist ideology lives on in the minds and hearts of any who hold onto the belief that Christian values are superior to all others and a belief that if we could help *"them"* be more like "*us*," all would be well.

I asked Lenny Christine, a Muslim woman in the Yumbe District of Uganda, why her community was so welcoming of refugees. She replied that it was Muslim religious teachings. Her religion, like Christianity, has been smeared by extremists who no more represent the core teachings of Islam than the Ku Klux Klan represents true Christianity.

WHAT IF we overcame our hubris and recognized that we have much to learn from the rest of the world, as Michael Moore showed in "Where to Invade Next?" People who suggest ways America could do better are often accused of being unpatriotic. I love my country, and because I want it to remain strong, I believe it is important to correct weaknesses and embrace opportunities for improvement. A famous quote, often attributed to Alex De Tocqueville, states that, "America is great because America is good. If America ever ceases to be good, America will cease to be great." The way to keep America great is to keep America on the path of truth, justice, fairness, and tolerance.

WHAT IF we tried to live up to the sentiments expressed on the Statue of Liberty and made the U.S. a welcome place with equal opportunity for all of "the world's huddled masses yearning to breathe free?"

WHAT IF P2P, Chris Roesel's non-profit, had funds for comprehensive water, sanitation, and health projects on a wide scale? It costs roughly $20,000 for a village of 500, and the ripple effects are significant, from increased work and school attendance to a near doubling of families' disposable income.

WHAT IF TCP Global had funding to support all Village Savings and Loan Associations (VSLAs) that, like the ones in Uganda, want to issue larger and more frequent loans than their small savings pool can provide? There are more than 67,000

VSLAs worldwide. TCP Global has worked with approximately 100 to date, and the waiting list is long.

WHAT IF Professor Ashe's Grassroots Finance Action (GFA) group had funds to incentivize savings groups in thousands of unbanked communities?

WHAT IF funds were available to replicate what HELP, the Maureen Orth Foundation, and EDUCATE TOMORROW have done in Haiti, Colombia and with former foster youth to make quality education widely available?

WHAT IF we banned guns instead of books and drag queens?

WHAT IF we allowed our full history to be taught so that we could learn from mistakes as well as achievements?

We are squandering opportunities to make the world a better, safer place for us all.

ACKNOWLEDGMENTS

Thanks to the first two presidents of the Rotary Club of Yumbe, Rukia Driciru and Lenny Christine and their amazing club members whose service in caring for humanity inspired this book.

Thanks to Avis Myers, who first edited the book, John Coyne, who provided guidance during the publishing effort and others from the St. Louis University community who financially supported TCP Global over the years: Brian and Mary Ternoey, Mike Flynn, Ann Marie Skinner Ruhlin, Michael Koetting, Tom and Agatha Brockland.

Thanks to Marian Haley Beil of Peace Corps Writers for shepherding me through the publication phase, to copyeditor Dimitra Manda, who made that part of the process a joy, and to Hassan Chaudhry of HMD Publishing for formatting my manuscript and designing the cover.

Thanks to many friends who painstakingly completed preliminary edits of the book: Susan Walton, Peggy Sievers Fagen, Pat O'Brien Dolan, and Glenn Blumhorst.

Thanks to Jeffrey Ashe for creating and leading the Thursday morning Grassroots Finance Action Zoom calls whose members are supportive, insightful, inspiring and who also care deeply about removing barriers from marginalized communities.

Thanks to the TCP Global Board, Curt Commander, Michelle Daniels, Chris Roesel, and Kathleen Schilb, who work hard to get resources to grassroots change-makers like the Yumbe Rotarians. Thank you also to past team members who shepherded The Colombia Project and then TCP Global through the first twenty-two years.

Thanks to all our TCP Global partners, especially Innocent Ajaga in Yumbe, Uganda; Zakari Hassane in Niger; Rita Arango,

Alejo Narvaez, Yasmila Altamar Caballero, Sister Ruby, Alba Lucia Moreno, and Ofelia Fernandez in Colombia,

Thank you to my family: Greg, Tim, Michele, and Julie Dudley, for their unwavering support and for giving me the green light to chip away at their inheritance to further the work of TCP Global.

Thanks to Rotarians Real Provencer Dave Snyder, Sparkie Folkers, Mary Walsh, James Willoughby, Steve Baker, and Ligia Corredor.

Thanks to our donors who have kept the dream alive, including Elizabeth Jenkins Joffee, Tony and Mary Ellen Eads, Betty Scalise, Vivian Morgan-Mendez, Susan Corcoran Hayes, Thomas and Patsy Lightbown, Steve Koch, Tim and Hyon O'Brien, Victor and Ruth Balestra, Sally Rowley and Tim Lawler.

Thank you to Zack Coen, Josh Concannon, Elyse Magen and all the other Peace Corps evacuees who used their COVID lock-down time to improve TCP Global.

Thank you to Coral Gables Congregational Church, Noah Clements, and Julio Leiva whose support at critical junctures kept The Colombia Project alive so it could evolve to TCP Global

Thanks to members of my two book clubs for their encouragement and financial support.

GLOSSARY

CBO - Community-based organization

CCEDUC - Care Community Education Centre - TCP Global partners in the Yumbe

District of Northern Uganda connection TCP Global to multiple VSLAs

DFN - Development Fund Norway, a nonprofit that supports CBOs in rural areas to assist marginalized people in remote areas of Nepal to improve their livelihoods and quality of life through training and entrepreneurial support.

DOCTRINE OF DISCOVERY – 15th-century papal proclamation justifying colonialist activities and subjugation of native populations.

GFA - Grassroots Finance Action - a group led by Columbia University Professor Jeffrey Ashe to discuss best practices for helping marginalized people improve their lives.

HELP - Haitian Education and Leadership Program was established by a former Peace Corps language instructor to provide education opportunities to Haitian scholars from impoverished backgrounds.

MUHAMMAD YUNUS - founder of the Grameen Bank and recipient of the 2006 Nobel Peace Prize for his work empowering the poor through micro-credit.

NGO - Non-governmental organization

NPCA - National Peace Corps Association, an alumni group of people who served with or supported the Peace Corps. It was TCP Global's fiscal sponsor from 2016-2022.

P2P - People to People, a nonprofit organization established by Returned Peace Corps Volunteer Rotarian Chris Roesel to provide low-cost solutions to water, sanitation, health, and hygiene problems.

PCV - Peace Corps Volunteer - someone currently serving in the Peace Corps

POTENTIEL TERRE – a nonprofit founded and led by Zakari Hassane to improve opportunities for impoverished people throughout Niger.

RPCV - Returned Peace Corps Volunteer - anyone who has served in the Peace Corps

SUSTAINABLE DEVELOPMENT GOALS - 17 goals adopted by the United Nations in 2015 as a shared blueprint for peace and prosperity for people and the planet.

TCP GLOBAL – the 2015 successor to The Colombia Project, continuing the same mission but on a global scale.

THE COLOMBIA PROJECT - a micro-loan program created in Colombia in 2000 with the dual mission of empowering impoverished entrepreneurs through affordable loans and strengthening effective grassroots organizations by establishing a revenue stream for their community projects.

VSLA - Village Savings and Loan Associations; membership groups of 30-50 people, usually women, who combine their weekly savings to give periodic loans to each other. When VSLAs want to issue more loans of larger amounts, many ask to join TCP Global.

WASH – Water, sanitation and hygiene

WHO - World Health Organization

Made in the USA
Coppell, TX
06 December 2023

25458381R00138